HOW COULD YOU, MRS. DICK?

DOUGLAS RODGER

The Glamourous Evelyn Dick - 1947

How Could You, Mrs. Dick? © Copyright 1989 Douglas Rodger

Playwrights Canada Press is the publishing imprint of
the Playwrights Union of Canada: 54 Wolseley St., 2nd fl.
Toronto, Ontario CANADA
M5T 1A5
Tel: (416) 947-0201
Fax: (416) 947-0159

Playwrights Canada Press operates with the generous assistance of
The Canada Council - Writing and Publishing Section, and Theatre Section,
and the Ontario Arts Council.

Front cover photo by Denise Grant.
Edited and designed by Tony Hamill.

Canadian Cataloguing in Publication Data
Douglas Rodger, 1950 -
    How could you, mrs. dick?
A play
ISBN 0-88754-483-5
I. Title.
PS8585.022H69 1992   C812'.54   C92-094423-X
PR9199.3.R622H69 1992

First edition: September 1992.
Printed and bound by Canadian Printco Ltd..

"Art is a lie which speaks the truth."

— *David Rosenfield*

To all those who encouraged me in writing this story over the last fifteen years, my thanks. To all those who attempted to discourage me, more thanks. Adversity is a great motivator. Lastly, to the thousands of people who bought tickets, who laughed and applauded — thank you for making the dream a reality.

— Douglas Rodger

AUTHOR'S NOTE

Everything stated in this play by a 'real' character, (EVELYN, ALEXANDRA, DONALD, JOHN DICK, WOOD and PRESTON) is based in verifiable fact, whether from trial transcripts, police reports, newspaper accounts, or my own original research. The only fictional characters are the two reporters but they are consistent with certain historical models and when they represent 'real' persons, such as John Dick or Anna Wolski, I have not invented their dialogue outright. However, I have granted myself some poetic licence.

STAGE DIRECTIONS

The phrase: **Change focus** indicates a new scene or a major shift in audience attention.

THE TORSO

The torso is headless and limbless, clad only in a suit of blue woolen Stanfield's combination underwear, an unusual type which has no buttons. (One steps in through the stretchable neck of the garment.) The clothing has been cut off with the limbs. What remains is bloody. The torso is of a man, 5' 10" in height and weighing approximately 185 lbs. The neck is severed at the 5th neck vertebra. The right arm is cut diagonally four and a half inches below the outside of the shoulder. The left arm has been severed transversely seven inches below the shoulder. The right leg is cut off 14 inches below the outer point of the hip; the left leg, six inches below the point of the hip. Across the belly, three inches above the navel, is a 12-inch gash, most of which has gone through the belly wall, perforating the bowel. In the central part of the right chest, an inch above the right nipple there are two gunshot wounds three and a half inches apart. The central one is an entry wound.

How Could You, Mrs Dick? was first produced by Theatre Terra Nova at the Studio Theatre of Hamilton Place, opening June 1st, 1989 with the following cast (in order of appearance):

KEITH EDWARDS	*Henry Czerny*
SGT. CLARENCE PRESTON	*Patrick Sinclair*
INSPECTOR CHARLES WOOD	*Lee J. Campbell*
ALEXANDRA MACLEAN	*Caroline Hetherington*
DONALD MACLEAN	*Harry Booker*
IRIS MUIRSON	*Nancy Palk*
EVELYN MACLEAN DICK	*Lesleh Donaldson*

Directed by Guy Sprung.
Designed by Jonathan Porter.
Lighting by Hatem Habashi.
Costumes by Eileen Earnshaw-Borghesan.
Produced by Brian Morton.
Stage Manager - Cindy Anderson.
Assistant Stage Manager- Barbara Wright.
Assistant Director - Jean Hughes.

The revised version of *How Could You, Mrs. Dick?* was produced by The Evelyn Group at the Tivoli Theatre in Hamilton and The Wintergarden Theatre in Toronto, October 7th to November 30th, 1991 with the following cast (in order of appearance):

Please note that in the revised version, an additional character, JOHN DICK, has been introduced to the play.

KEITH EDWARDS	*Maurice Godin*
IRIS MUIRSON	*Barbara Gordon*
SGT. CLARENCE PRESTON	*Patrick Sinclair*
INSPECTOR CHARLES WOOD	*David Ferry*
ALEXANDRA MACLEAN	*Caroline Hetherington*
DONALD MACLEAN	*Ted Johns*
EVELYN MACLEAN DICK	*Lesleh Donaldson*
JOHN DICK	*Lubomir Mykytiuk*

Directed by Guy Sprung.
Designed by Jonathan Porter.
Lighting by Graeme Thomson.
Music composed by Ron Lewis Jacobson.
Costumes by Denyse Cronenberg.
Production Manager - Brian Morton.
Stage Manager - Anne Putnam.
Assistant Stage Manager - Thelma Phillips.

The Characters (in order of appearance)

KEITH EDWARDS — *Early Twenties, single, Hamilton native, an enthusiastic hack writer trying to make his name.*

IRIS MUIRSON — *Fortyish, well-bred, attractive, educated abroad, one of the nation's top female journalists.*

DET. SGT. CLARENCE PRESTON — *Sixtyish, 25-year veteran of the Hamilton Police Department, Northern English accent. Rough around the edges.*

INSPECTOR CHARLES WOOD — *Forties, Toronto-born, 20-year veteran of the Ontario Provincial Police, small in stature, well-dressed.*

MRS. ALEXANDRA MACLEAN — *Sixty, Aberdeen Scot, slender, severe, formerly a nurse in a psychiatric hospital, wife of Donald MacLean, mother of Evelyn.*

MRS. EVELYN DICK — *Twenty-five, attractive with dark hair and eyes, daughter of Alexandra and Donald, married to John Dick.*

DONALD MACLEAN — *Sixty-four, Glaswegian, a Hamilton Street Railway janitor, stocky, alcoholic, explosive temper, married to Alexandra, father of Evelyn.*

JOHN DICK — *Forty, a Mennonite, placid, naive, employed as Hamilton Street Railway motorman, lifelong bachelor until marriage to Evelyn.*

ACT ONE

*Lights up on the press room of the
Supreme Court building. A shabby,
littered office. It is April 3rd, 1947
according to the bank calendar on the
wall. There are wooden chairs and a
battered radio on a file cabinet. A
radiator against the upstage wall
occassionally hisses and clanks. There is
a table dead-centre stage and desks on
both downstage sides, one Keith's and
one Iris'. INSPECTOR WOOD's desk
is upstage right. Each desk has a handset
telephone.*

*Another table is against the upstage
wall under a large map of Hamilton. All
the important locations of the story
have been marked and identified by the
out-of-town reporters. The upstage table
is used for evidence.*

*A cafe table and a bentwood chair, up
left, is DONALD MACLEAN's regular
spot at the Balmoral tavern. The only
door is up right beside WOOD's desk
and the coat tree. The only window is in
the shape of a large arch. A wooden
hand rail acts as a witness box and there
are two chairs behind it, one of them
ALEXANDRA's 'station'. There are
newspapers, magazines, clippings,
courtroom sketches and deritus
everywhere.*

*Big band music plays on a small radio.
KEITH enters, wet, cigarette in mouth,
and hat soggy with snow. He's shabby
dressed but has energy and a sleazy
charm. He looks around, pleased to have
the room to himself, takes off his hat
and jacket.*

ANNOUNCER   It's a quarter past nine in Hamilton and you're
listening to CKOC. That's quite the spring
blizzard outside. The Dominion Motor Club
warns that Lakeshore Road is closed just past
The Brant Inn in Burlington. For your own
safety, don't venture out on the roads tonight.

*KEITH takes a bottle of milk from the
radiator where it's been heating and
pours some into a cup at his desk. He
dumps in a mound of Ovaltine, drops in
some sugar cubes from his pockets and
stirs the contents with his fingers.*

KEITH   Suppertime. Come and get it.*(gulping it down in
one long swallow)*

ANNOUNCER   Before we get back to your favourite music,
brought to you by Firth Brother's Quality
Tailors, I have a special guest: top reporter, Dave
"Scoop" Woodruff. What's the scoop, Dave?

*KEITH pulls out a TRUE CRIME
magazine with EVELYN on the cover.*

KEITH   Dave Woodruff doesn't have the cover of *True
Crime* magazine - Keith Edwards does.

*KEITH goes to the radio near IRIS'
desk then picks up a photograph of a
child.*

WOODRUFF	Mark this day in your diary, Hamilton; April the third, 1947; today, the most sensational murder case in Canadian history wound up right here in Hamilton; I'm talking about The Torso Murder Case.
ANNOUNCER	I understand you'll have a special report for us.
WOODRUFF	Listen in, Sunday at six, folks, you'll get the inside scoop on the Dick murder, the last word on our notorious femme fatale, Evelyn Dick. The out-of-town press have skedaddled but I'm still here! And who can tell it better than me. This is Dave Woodruff reporting.
ANNOUNCER	Thanks, Dave. Maestro, music please!
KEITH	Kiss my Royal Canadian! Dave Woodruff don't know shit from Shin-ola.
	IRIS MUIRSON enters the press room. She is good-looking, and smartly dressed, about 40. KEITH is unaware. Setting her purse and briefcase down, she slips off her coat and hat. She is amused at KEITH's antics.
IRIS	I'm not sure he can hear you.
KEITH	(*startled*) You always sneak around like that?
IRIS	Do you live here now? (*seeing milk and Ovaltine*) On the hard stuff I see.
	KEITH slips the picture back on her desk, playing the innocent. IRIS picks up the photo with a sharp, knowing glance at him.
KEITH	She's quite a looker. Is she your daughter?
IRIS	You know perfectly well I'm not married. Celeste is my niece.

> IRIS *fits a cigarette into a long holder
> and lights it. As she speaks on the
> phone, she sense* KEITH's *mimicry*

IRIS Operator, a collect call please. To Toronto, Empire 7614. From Iris Muirson...Yes. Thank you operator. (*louder for* KEITH's *benefit*) I'm delighted you read my column. (*pause*) Transcription please. (*bringing out a note pad*) Hello Ralph...Iris here. Yes I was going to drive in but...the storm, I won't get through. No, I've checked out of the Connaught. I'm in the Press Room at the Courthouse. Ready? "Hamilton, Ontario, April 3/47. (*dictating*) Forever I swear when I hear the hissing and clanking of a steam pipe I shall think of Evelyn Dick, comma...

> KEITH *slams his metal ashtray in the
> wastebasket,* IRIS *glares at him as he
> grins impishly.*

IRIS (*jumping ahead*)...Evelyn Dick with her strange calm, comma, sitting on that long hard mahogany bench day after day, period. I shall remember the strange face with its black sullen eyes and the full lower lip protruding with peevish impotence Period. I shall remember...Damn! The phone's gone out!

KEITH Forever I swear, I shall remember never to write 'I shall remember'. Period.

IRIS Don't lecture me on writing Mr. Edwards. I've read your lurid trash.

> IRIS *picks up his TRUE CRIME
> magazine and leafs through it.*

IRIS "Evelyn Dick The Tragic Story of an Emotional Degenerate." Very subtle.

KEITH Of course, you're a graduate of the University of La-di-da on the Thames.

IRIS	(*reading*) Oh, readers, here is a tragedy of twisted lives, of crazy, crawling desires, of blind, grinding, intolerable urges, secrets and sighs..." Where did you learn to fashion such purple prose?
KEITH	I went to Delta.
IRIS	Fascinating. Operator! (*banging the phone*) Delta? Is that a Reform School?
KEITH	Delta Collegiate.
IRIS	Really! Why not wear the old school tie? What is it, a noose? Hello, yes, operator I was cut off.. Oh, the wires are down, of course. The storm. When will they be restored? I have a deadline. I shall stay by this phone, all night if need be. The number is 2-7949. Call me the moment the line is open. Thank you...What? (*pause*) Yes of course, but another time perhaps. (*hanging up*)
KEITH	She's got an Evelyn story, right?
IRIS	Doesn't everyone in this bizarre backwater have an Evelyn story? The poor souls are proud of her!
KEITH	Her old man was a janitor who stole his employer blind. She spent money like a drunken sailor, screwed half the city, never did an honest day's work and then bumped off her hubby. This is Hamilton; of course we're proud of her.
IRIS	She put your little town on the front page.
	KEITH *holds up the magazine with* EVELYN *on the cover.*
KEITH	This is the first Canadian cover story *True Crime* ever ran.
IRIS	(*à la Lorne Greene*) A nation comes of age!

KEITH	Now I'm writing a book. Her story is gonna be my ticket out of here.
IRIS	Not a book - an opus, surely! You have a commission?
KEITH	Not yet.
IRIS	I see. (*relieved*) So, you're going to take advantage of her misfortune.
KEITH	That's rich coming from a sob sister.
IRIS	I am a newspaperman not a tabloid scribbler.
KEITH	You dish up the dirt too. I've read your polite but maudlin trash.
IRIS	Ouch.
KEITH	Why not write a book? I've almost got the case cracked. (*puffed up*) See, I've done a bit of amateur sleuthing.
IRIS	Sleuthing! Why, you could be the next Franklin W. Dixon! The Hardy Boys and the Mystery of the Truncated Torso.
KEITH	Don't be so (*mispronouncing*) facile.
IRIS	That's facile, as in smug and supercilious.

> KEITH *turns away stony-faced and pounds on the typewriter.* IRIS *pulls a flask from her purse and pours herself a drink. He sneaks a greedy glance, meets her eyes and arch smile.*

IRIS	Help yourself.

> KEITH *wipes his mug on his tie and is at her desk in a flash pouring a drink.*

IRIS	You are old enough, I presume.
KEITH	(*lifting his glass in a toast to her*) Scotch! La verrai chose - as they say in Paris, Ontario.
IRIS	(*toasting*) So, Mr. Edwards..
KEITH	Call me Keith.
IRIS	Keith. Please, call me Miss Muirson. So you think Evelyn Dick murdered her husband.
KEITH	Sure, don't you?
IRIS	No, I don't.
KEITH	Well. You're the only one.
IRIS	Me and the jury.
KEITH	So, who did it then?
IRIS	Here's an opening sentence for your book - free of charge. "After a long series of trials and retrials, it can now be said conclusively, that John Dick did not commit suicide, dismember himself and throw his own remains off the mountain." All else is conjecture.
KEITH	I bet I can change your mind.
IRIS	About what?
KEITH	Lots of things. Me, for instance. You think I'm a pushy little low life...
IRIS	That's more thought than I've given you.
KEITH	I saw you last week, giving me the once-over. (*making a too-obvious pass*).

IRIS	You've mistaken bemused incredulity for amorous interest. Restrain yourself or you're cut off.
KEITH	Okay.
	KEITH *lifts a heavy metal box and drops it on his desk.*
KEITH	See this? I got files in here, transcripts, secret cop reports, interviews, info I picked up. So let's just look at the facts -- I'll change your mind about Mrs. Dick.
IRIS	I might change yours.
KEITH	Come on, get serious. You like to gamble, I seen you play poker with Dave Woodruff and the boys.
IRIS	That wasn't gambling. Did you ever see me lose?
KEITH	(*shrugging*) So make me a little wager? If I convince you she's guilty, you buy me dinner. If you're not persuaded, the meal is on me.
IRIS	(*droll*) Oh splendid. Either way I lose.
KEITH	You're afraid to face the truth. (*holding up his manuscript*) My rough draft. To quote the Bard: "Here, here upon this bank and shoal of time, I have cut through the flesh of speculation and exposéd the bone of truth." (*stressing last 'ed"*)
IRIS	Macbeth. And you didn't quote the Bard - you butcheréd him. Pardon the expression. Go ahead and present your case. I' can't go anywhere.
	KEITH *reads from notes with delight.*
KEITH	I have dedicated this tome to the detectives on this case, Sgt. Clarence Preston, Grizzled Veteran of the Hamilton Police Department.

Change focus: PRESTON *enters. He is in his late 50's, slightly shabby, wearing an overcoat and Fedora.*

KEITH

"His features might seem grim and sour if not for the animated sparkle in his shrewd perceptive eyes. Preston had pulled Homicide Duty on the 16th of March 1946. A day like any other - until a call came in. A group of kids out for a wholesome hike on the Mountainside had discovered the butchered remains of what was once a man."

Lights up on a realistic, bloody torso, lying breast down. PRESTON *moves to it and stares at it.*

KEITH

The body was found here, near Albion Falls (*at map*) in OPP jurisdiction. (*reading*) "Assigned to crack the case, was Ace Homicide Detective, Inspector Charles Wood; a dogged, thorough shamus with a fanatical flair for minute detail."

WOOD *enters wearing a conservative, expensive suit and overcoat. He is 40, with dark hair, glasses, and a pipe. He studies the torso for a moment and then extends his hand to* PRESTON.

WOOD

Are you Hamilton P.D.?

PRESTON

I am. Detective Sergeant Clarence Preston. (*shaking hands*)

WOOD

Inspector Charles Wood, OPP Criminal Investigations Branch.

PRESTON

Yeah, I've heard of you.

WOOD

The Commissioner's assigned me to head this investigation.

PRESTON

Is that so?

WOOD	Yes. (*conciliatory*) We'll work together. Have you done many murders?
PRESTON	No. Morality's my beat. Bootleggers and bookies.
WOOD	Murder's my specialty.
PRESTON	Like old Sherlock Holmes, sir.
WOOD	That's just malarkey. I am the real thing.

> WOOD *crouches, studying the torso. He lights his pipe and indicates being on a steep slope.*

PRESTON	You see the path, how it slid down here, head first, pardon sir, and caught on the saplings.
WOOD	Yes. (*sniffing*) The brush and weeds have almost straightened up again. It's been here for a while. Who is he?
PRESTON	No idea. We're checking. Looks like a mob job.
WOOD	You get your share of those here, don't you?
PRESTON	(*grimacing and pausing*) What are you looking for?
WOOD	Anything. Everything. You only get one crack at the scene of a murder. You'll never be here, like this again. Look at these serrations on the flesh of the neck - his head was probably severed with an ordinary saw. Likewise the limbs. Whoever it was, he got tired of sawing through this arm bone and forced it the rest of the way. Snapped it like a piece of wood.

> KEITH *snaps a pencil in half on the last line, startling* IRIS.

KEITH	Geez, I'm really sorry.

WOOD	Turn him over.
	WOOD *tamps his pipe and lets* PRESTON *do the work.*
	Change focus to KEITH *and* IRIS.
IRIS	What was the official cause of death?
KEITH	(*getting file*) I've got the pathologist's report.
IRIS	Ah, the aptly named Doctor Deadman, a name Dickens would have used.
KEITH	(*skimming*) There was no evidence of fatal injury to the torso so we assume that the death resulted from some fatal injury to the head...
IRIS	...which they never found.
	Change focus to police and torso.
WOOD	They had an idea here to cut through the stomach but obviously gave up.
PRESTON	Look sir, two bullet holes! He was shot twice!
WOOD	Once, at close range. This is the entry wound, see the powder burn? This is the exit. That didn't kill him.
	PRESTON *and* KEITH *drag the torso upstage and cover it with a sheet.*
KEITH	Nobody knows who the stiff is. The papers figure maybe it's Rocco Perri.
IRIS	Oh yes, your famous mobster.
KEITH	Rocco took a walk four years ago and he ain't back yet. It took almost three days to identify the torso.

Change focus to WOOD *and*
PRESTON *at office.*

PRESTON   Umm, Inspector...

WOOD   Yes. (*staring*)

PRESTON   (*uneasy*) Regarding the i.d. of the torso, there's another Missing Person's Report.

WOOD   Just come in?

PRESTON   No sir. It was actually made last week before the body was found. It just got misfiled.

WOOD   Oh for Christsake. Well, give me the details.

PRESTON   There's a fella, a motorman works for the Hamilton Street Railway, name of John Dick, been missing for about ten or twelve days.

WOOD   Who reported him missing?

PRESTON   His cousin, Alex Kammerer. Dick was a Mennonite from a farm family down Grimsby way. Moved up here to work in town. He's been staying at the Kammerer house since he split up with his wife.

WOOD   A Mennonite breaking up with his wife?

PRESTON   Something else, sir, last...Tuesday the 12th. John Dick's estranged wife, a Mrs. Evelyn Dick, came in to the Station and reported him missing. She said her husband took off with tickets and money belonging to the Hamilton Street Railway and they were after her to pay it back.

WOOD   If our torso is this Dick fellow, we'll have a word with his wife.

KEITH	March 19, 1946. Noon hour. At the solid, middle-class, brick house, number 32 Carrick Avenue, Mrs. Alexandra MacLean hears a knock at the door. (*knocking*)
	Change focus *to* WOOD *and* PRESTON. ALEXANDRA MACLEAN *enters, 60, severe, Scottish.*
KEITH	She's a brisk, determined, little lady with a frosty Aberdeen air.
	ALEXANDRA *'opens' the door for* WOOD *and* PRESTON.
ALEXANDRA	Mr. Preston. Good day.
PRESTON	Oh! Good day, Mrs.. MacLean.
ALEXANDRA	What can I do for you?
PRESTON	Is your daughter at home?
ALEXANDRA	Yes. She's having lunch.
PRESTON	This is Inspector Wood of the Ontario Provincial Police.
WOOD	I'd like to speak with Mrs. Dick.
	ALEXANDRA *moves away.* WOOD *and* PRESTON *talk togrether.*
WOOD	You know them?
PRESTON	Yes, I didn't connect the names. I know the family casually, to say hello. Her old man, Donald MacLean works as a janitor.

	DONALD MACLEAN *enters in his work clothes, 60ish, heavyset, florid, and gloomy. He lumbers to his Balmoral table.*
KEITH	Donald MacLean, A Demonic Drinker with a terrible temper and a soft spot for his dark-eyed daughter. You could find him any night at the Balmoral Tavern, asleep in his beer.
KEITH	(*as* WAITER *shaking* DONALD) Come on Don. Time to go.
DONALD	(*as if being woken up still drunk*) Ohh! Aye.. Aye Eddie, aye. Time t'go. Gie us a ride home, will you? (*gripping* KEITH *fiercely*) Where's ma Evelyn? She's ma wee pet. Ha' you seen ma wee pet, Eddie?
	Change focus *to* WOOD *and* PRESTON *at Carrick Avenue.*
WOOD	Where does he work?
PRESTON	At the Hamilton Street Railway.
WOOD	The same company John Dick worked for?
PRESTON	(*the penny drops*) Right.
	Change focus *to* ALEXANDRA *at the up-centre doorway.* EVELYN *enters the 'kitchen' to meet her mother. She is 26, wearing an expensive dress, well made-up with lustrous black hair and dark, appealing eyes.*
KEITH	Enter, the beautiful, enigmatic central character, a dark vibrant woman of undeniable fascination, her wondrous eyes too bright with living.

KEITH	She had drained life's glittering cup to the bitter dregs but her essential femininity still moistened the eyes of men. Her name was ...
ALEXANDRA	Evelyn, it's the police. They want to speak to you.
	EVELYN *looks at her blankly as her mother prepares her to meet the police.*
ALEXANDRA	What will you tell them?
	EVELYN *doesn't ansewr but walks to* WOOD *and* PRESTON.
EVELYN	(*smiling warmly*) Clarence, hello.
PRESTON	Hello.
EVELYN	(*to* WOOD) Hi.
WOOD	Good day. Are you Mrs. Evelyn Dick?
EVELYN	Yes. (*moving closer to him, smiling and waiting for* WOOD *to light her cigarette which he does*)
WOOD	My name is Inspector Charles Wood of the Ontario Provincial Police, Criminal Investigations Branch. (*pause*) Are you the wife of John Dick?
EVELYN	Well I am but we're separated. I haven't seen him for a while. He's a driver for the Street Railway. He's got bond money and car tickets belonging to the company and they've been after me for it.
WOOD	I see.
	EVELYN *smokes,* WOOD *watches -- cat and mouse.*
WOOD	When did you last see your husband?

EVELYN	Around two weeks ago.
WOOD	That would be Monday, March the fourth?
EVELYN	I think so.
WOOD	Mrs. Dick, you have probably read in the paper of the finding of a torso on the mountain last Saturday?

> WOOD *expects an answer but* EVELYN *stares at him impassively.*

WOOD	I'm afraid I have bad news, Mrs. Dick. That torso has been identified as the body of your husband.
EVELYN	(*eyes flaring*) Don't look at me, I don't know anything about it.
WOOD	You better get your coat and we'll go down to Central Station. Just to talk this over.

> EVELYN *takes her coat from the coat tree.*

WOOD	Clarence, there's something she's not telling us.
PRESTON	Pretty little thing like that, I can't see her mixed up in a murder.

> ***Change focus*** *to* IRIS *and* KEITH.

IRIS	Why was Donald there when the police arrived? He and his wife were separated.
KEITH	He was visiting, I guess. His place at 214 Rosslyn, it's not far away from Carrick Avenue.

> ***Change focus*** *to* DONALD *approaching* PRESTON.

DONALD	Clarence, what d'ye want with my daughter? Is she in some sort o' trouble?

PRESTON	Go on back home Donald, she's not been charged with anything.
DONALD	She never done nothin'.
PRESTON	We're just going to talk to her.
DONALD	She ought to have a lawyer.
PRESTON	If she didn't do anything, why does she need a lawyer?
	Change focus to interrogation table. EVELYN *makes her way to the centre table, swirls her skirt and sits down showing off her legs.*
IRIS	Every time she came through a door, it was an entrance. When you met her gaze, she'd never turn away first.
KEITH	Once in Court, our eyes met, hers and mine.
	KEITH *and* EVELYN's *eyes meet. She stretches her legs sensually.*
KEITH	I will never forget those eyes. You know what she'd do? She'd pick one of the jurors, and just watch him, concentrate on him, fantasize see, till she attained an unspeakable ecstasy.
	EVELYN *trembles orgasmically.*
IRIS	That is both speculative and smutty. Suitable grist for the *True Crime* mill.
KEITH	No, it's true!
IRIS	Have you ever seen a woman have a climax?
KEITH	(*shrugging*) Oh sure. (*lying*)

IRIS   Really? Perhaps at this very moment, looking at you, I'm attaining a 'blind, grinding, unspeakable ecstasy'.

KEITH   Okay, okay!

IRIS   It was probably indigestion.

              Change focus to the interrogation table. EVELYN *smokes constantly - unfiltered Sweet Caporals from a flat tin of 50. She picks the odd thread of tobacco from her tongue. At times she langourously dons a pair of black gloves lying on the table. At other times she moves uneasily, playing with the gloves. She removes her shoes and stretches her legs.*

              WOOD *takes a seat across from her but often walks about.* PRESTON *records the interview.*

WOOD   Sgt. Preston will take down whatever we say.

EVELYN   Fine.

WOOD   Are you comfortable?

EVELYN   Yes.

WOOD   Your name is Mrs. Evelyn Grant Dick?

EVELYN   Yes, right.

WOOD   Where do you live Mrs. Dick?

EVELYN   32 Carrick Avenue.

WOOD   You are married, I believe?

EVELYN   Yes. The 4th of October.

WOOD	What year?
EVELYN	Last year, 1945.
WOOD	Who was your husband?
EVELYN	John Dick.
KEITH	And finally, John Dick, Doomed Motorman on a trolley ride to death.

> *Change focus to* JOHN DICK *and* EVELYN *at HSR office where she has imaginary 4-year-old daughter, Heather, in tow.* JOHN *enters wearing an HSR uniform with a money changer and punch on his belt. His hair is sandy-brown and he has a slight German accent. He is a 'ghost' character - his presence is often felt in scenes where he is silent.*

JOHN	Hello.
EVELYN	Hi.
JOHN	She is your daughter?
EVELYN	Yes, she is.
JOHN	Hello, Heather. She is pretty, I think, like her mother.
EVELYN	That's kind of you to say so.
JOHN	Uhh, can I help you?
EVELYN	Yes, I'm looking for my father. Donald McLean.
JOHN	I don't know him.
EVELYN	The janitor? He's been here twenty years eh?

JOHN	(*taken aback*) Him? He is your father?
EVELYN	(*terse*) Yes.
JOHN	He's probably cleaning up in the counting room. You like a peppermint, Heather?
EVELYN	You're awfully good with kids. Do you have any?
JOHN	Me? No, no. I'm not married.
EVELYN	What's your name?
JOHN	I'm John Dick. I drive the Number 20 Belt Line.

EVELYN *smiles at* JOHN *warmly.*

KEITH	"And with just such a glance from woman is a man's fate sealed in the stars".

***Change focus** to interrogation.*

WOOD	Mrs. Dick, you are being detained in connection with your husband's death. You are not obliged to make any statement unless you wish to do so but whatever you say is being taken down and may be used as evidence. Do you understand that?
EVELYN	Yes, I understand.
WOOD	You and your husband were not living together?
EVELYN	That is correct.
WOOD	When did you separate?
EVELYN	Does that mean Dec. 24 or the last time he stepped into the house?
WOOD	I mean the day he left you.
EVELYN	December 24.

Change focus to JOHN *and* EVELYN *with* ALEXANDRA *hovering nearby.*

ALEXANDRA   You needn't leave in broad daylight for the neighbours to see.

JOHN   Why do you care what neighbours think? (*to* EVELYN) You want me to stay, throw out your mother. Tell her to go back to her husband.

EVELYN   Where are you going to stay? In case I have to forward any mail.

JOHN   To Mrs. Kammerer. Don't you laugh, old missus. You are not get rid of me so easy.

Change focus to interrogation.

WOOD   You know that the torso found on the mountainside was that of your husband. What can you tell me about that?

EVELYN   Well, I have known he was running around with women. I have seen him myself with other women. A well-dressed man I took to be an Italian *(Eyetalian)* came to the door and asked if John were in. I said no. He said John was breaking his home up and he would like him to lay off visiting her or he would fix him and I said, 'What do you mean?' He said, 'We fix him, all right, one way or the other.. get him sooner or later.

WOOD   Do you know who that man is?

EVELYN   I know he is a well-dressed man and I take it he is Italian. *(Eyetalian)*

WOOD   He spoke like an Italian?

EVELYN   Yes. Beautiful pearl teeth, a heavy filling of gold and a gold cap here and on the other side here.

EVELYN   He had a bowler hat, a dark overcoat and a flashy
          tie. Beautifully dressed and quite a flashy diamond
          ring in a claw setting.

WOOD   Could you pick out this man's picture, do you
          think?

EVELYN   Say down at Sherman and Burlington or James
          North I could pick him out.

IRIS   What is it about your North End? It seems to be
          peopled with characters from the back lot of
          Warner Brothers.

KEITH   Easy sister. That's my old stomping grounds.

IRIS   My point exactly.

WOOD   Had you made any plans beforehand with this
          Italian fellow, to do away with your husband?

EVELYN   No, but I heard John was going to be fixed, one
          way or the other.

          Change focus as JOHN DICK *enters
          the hotel room.*

WOOD   Since your husband left in December, did you
          spend a night with him at The Royal Connaught
          Hotel?

EVELYN   Yes.

          Change focus to EVELYN *and*
          JOHN.

JOHN   (*on phone*) Hello Mrs. Kammerer. I will not be
          home for all weekend. I am staying at The Royal
          Connaught with my wife. She give me twenty-
          five dollars to pay for such an expensive place.

          JOHN *hangs up as* EVELYN *comes to
          his side.*

JOHN	It's nice we are alone without your mother to interfere.
EVELYN	Have a Scotch, John. (*pouring* JOHN *a large tumbler*)
JOHN	Not so much.
EVELYN	Come on, don't you want to have fun?
JOHN	You want to get me drunk so there will be no talk about our problems.
EVELYN	What problems?
JOHN	You know what I mean.
EVELYN	John, you'd better stop scandalizing my name all over town. (*sexy*) Drink up and come to bed.

> JOHN *grabs a petulant, glowering* EVELYN *by the arm.*

JOHN	Evelyn, the time is getting short and you had better come to live with me or else you will have to appear in Court and they will find out you married me under a phony name.
EVELYN	John, don't do that. We'll get a place together as soon as Heather is well again.

> EVELYN *kisses* JOHN *lasciviously but after a moment he pulls back.*

JOHN	(*angry but passionate*) Always there is some story from you. I can't believe a word you say.
IRIS	She wanted to patch things up.
KEITH	That wasn't affection. She was trying to control him.

Change focus *to interrogation.*

WOOD	Do you drive a car?
EVELYN	No.
WOOD	Do you drive a car?
EVELYN	You mean can I drive a car?
WOOD	Yes.
EVELYN	Yes.
WOOD	Do you own a car of your own?
EVELYN	No.
WOOD	Have you borrowed a car lately?
EVELYN	Yes.
WOOD	From whom?
EVELYN	Grafton Garage. Mister Landeg.
WOOD	I believe he bought a car from you some years ago?
EVELYN	No, I gave it to him because it was costing me too much of an expense.
IRIS	Wood knew the answer before he asked the question.
KEITH	It's one way to find out if she's lying.
WOOD	This car you borrowed, this was the same car? A black, 1938 Packard two-door sedan?
EVELYN	Yes.
WOOD	What day would that be?
EVELYN	The sixth.

WOOD	Wednesday, March the sixth.
EVELYN	Yes.
WOOD	Tell us about your movements on that day?
EVELYN	I borrowed the car to do some shopping.
WOOD	Where did you go?
EVELYN	Garvin Hardware, Eatons, The Liberty Shop, The Bronx Shoe Store. Then I went home, say, a quarter to five.
WOOD	Did anything unusual happen that evening?
EVELYN	Yes, a phone call.
WOOD	From whom?
EVELYN	A member of a gang from Windsor.
WOOD	A member of what gang from Windsor? Do you know their names?
EVELYN	Just their first names. He said -- he asked for me, it was my mother answered the phone and I said, "Hello" and he said, 'This is one of the gang speaking. We caught up with your husband. He was warned to lay off a friend of mine's wife and he has left her in the family way. So we've been paid to put John out of business'.
WOOD	He told you all of this over the telephone?
EVELYN	Yes, officer, he did. Well, he didn't perhaps use such poor grammar as I did but to put him out of the way. He said I would like to meet you tonight: "Can you borrow a car?" "Well," I said, "not for long" so he met me at the old James Street Incline.

Movie music under following sequence.

EVELYN   There was a car there, a black Oldsmobile or a black Buick, 1941 or 42, a beautiful car parked in the dark at the edge of Claremont Drive. I drove up and there was a man standing at the side of the car.

WOOD   So this was the same man who had come to the house earlier to complain about John visiting his wife?

EVELYN   No, it wasn't.

WOOD   What was said or done from there?

EVELYN   Well, he had this sack with him.

WOOD   Was there anything in it?

EVELYN   Yes.

WOOD   Was it heavy?

EVELYN   Yes.

WOOD   Was this man carrying the sack?

EVELYN   No, he was pulling it. He said he wanted to get rid of this quick. I said you had better not use this car. He said, "Get in and put on the speed".

WOOD   What did he do with the sack?

EVELYN   He put it in the front seat to begin with and then pushed it over to the back. He said "Come on, I haven't got much time," and I was scared all the time.

WOOD   Did he tell you what was in the sack?

EVELYN   Yes. He said part of John.

WOOD   What else did he say?

EVELYN	We weren't talking there for a while when we went along Concession Street and out towards Albion Falls. He said hurry up, drive faster and he kept putting his foot over top of mine because I drove too slow. He said pull over and let me drive. So I did and he got behind the wheel.
WOOD	Where did he drive you?
EVELYN	Just further along the Mountain Brow to where he stopped.
WOOD	The place you stopped, was this before you got to Albion Falls?
EVELYN	Well, I know it is on the road, that is all, near a bend like and if you were at this side of the bend you go around the bend and you see the cars disappearing down you think (*smiling as if all is perfectly clear*).
KEITH	That's a pretty good description of the spot where the body was found.
IRIS	*The Spectator* printed a map. She could have gotten this story for a nickel at the newsstand.
WOOD	What did this man do next?
EVELYN	He took the bag off him. He pulled the bag off and when I saw the torso, I took sick and vomited. He grabbed the torso, ran across the road and rolled him down the bank. He threw the bag in the car and tossed it out coming back.
WOOD	(*to* EVELYN) You drove down the Mountain. Then what did you do?
EVELYN	I drove to the Connaught Hotel and let him off.
WOOD	Where did you go then?

EVELYN	To the Grafton Garage to bring the car back.
WOOD	What time would that be?
EVELYN	I couldn't say roughly.
PRESTON	(*aside to* WOOD) The night man at the Grafton Garage said she brought the car back about 7:30 that night and left a note. He got blood on his hands when he moved the car. We found this tie in the back seat. It's bloodstained, sir, and still knotted.
WOOD	How did you feel when he told you it was part of John in the bag?
EVELYN	Well, I just can't express how I felt.
WOOD	Were you glad your husband was being done away with?
EVELYN	Well, no, but it was a pretty mean trick to break up a home.
WOOD	But he was your husband?
EVELYN	Yes, but he had so many enemies.
IRIS	What a strange match: her and a forty-year-old Mennonite?
	Change focus *to continutation of same scene with* JOHN *and* EVELYN *at HSR yard.*
JOHN	I drive the number 20 Belt Line.
EVELYN	(*extending her gloved hand*) Pleased to meet you. I'm Evelyn White. You got a steady John?
JOHN	(*startled*) No, no.
EVELYN	Come on, good-looking guy like you?

JOHN   (*guilty*) No, I don't.

EVELYN   It's hard being on your own right? (*confiding*) I'm
              a war widow myself.

JOHN   (*delighted*) I'm sorry to hear.

EVELYN   He was an Admiral in the R.C.N. Torpedoed off
              Malta. He went down with his ship.

JOHN   What ship was that?

EVELYN   The *H.M.C.S. Balmoral.*

JOHN   You must be so proud.

EVELYN   (*brightly*) Yes. (*smiling warmly and
              consistently*)

JOHN   (*at a loss for words*) I...I get your father.

EVELYN   (*moving very close*) John, I live in Henson Park
              Manor, third floor. Drop by for a coffee
              sometime.

JOHN   (*thrilled*) Sure.

                    JOHN *turns and almost collides with*
                    DONALD *who glares. at him.*

DONALD   (*to* EVELYN) Aye. What d'ye want?

EVELYN   Bye, John.

JOHN   Goodbye Mrs. White.

                    JOHN *exits unaware of* DONALD's *dark
                    glance.*

EVELYN   How are things with you?

DONALD   Pretty quiet since you lot left.

EVELYN	I need some money, a thou or so.
DONALD	(*snorting*) Aye. Did her send you? Her with thousands in the bank?

> EVELYN *sighs with exasperation -- this is an old argument.*

DONALD	No' here, it's nae safe. Come round the house later, I'll gie it you there.
EVELYN	Can I use the car?
DONALD	No.

> **Change focus** *to* IRIS *and* KEITH, *as he unzips* EVELYN's *dress which she removes.*

KEITH	She married John because she needed a respectable front. The war widow act was wearing pretty thin. She bought the Admiral's picture out of a store window. (*miming the Admiral going down with the ship*)
IRIS	Maybe Evelyn just found John loveable.
KEITH	Then she should have bought a puppy.

> **Change focus** *to Henson Park Manor. There is a knock at the door.* EVELYN *wears a slip.*

EVELYN	(*sleepily*) Who is it?
JOHN	(*offstage*) Mrs. White, it's John Dick.
EVELYN	Who?
JOHN	(*offstage*) We met yesterday. You said to drop by.
EVELYN	What time is it?

JOHN   (*offstage*) One o'clock...in the afternoon. I
                brought you something. A present.

                        The door opens to reveal JOHN,
                        nervous and excited. He offers a brown
                        paper package which EVELYN eagerly
                        takes.

EVELYN   Hi. Sorry, I couldn't place the name. Come on
                in.

                        JOHN enters, closing the door and
                        taking his hat off.

EVELYN   What'd you bring me?

                        EVELYN opens the package to reveal a
                        blue box of LUX Soapflakes.

EVELYN   Soapflakes! (*genuinely pleased*) That's very
                thoughtful John. (*impusively kissing him*)

EVELYN   You can't get these for love or money.

JOHN   (*blushing*) I got a friend at Lever Brother's can
                get as much as you need.

EVELYN   They'll come in real handy.

JOHN   Where is Heather?

EVELYN   Out with mother.

JOHN   Your mother lives here?

EVELYN   Yeah. She's separated from my father. Well, he
                drinks like a fish.

JOHN   I see him that way at the work sometime.

                        EVELYN's mood swings down for a
                        moment.

JOHN	This is nice, this place.
EVELYN	Too small for three of us. Sit down.
JOHN	Thank you. It must be expensive.
EVELYN	Yes. Norman, my husband, he left me very well off. His family was in the money from stocks and bonds and so on. He himself was a stockbroker. We got married down in Cleveland. What a do, we really put on the dog.
JOHN	He was American?
EVELYN	Yes, he came up here as a volunteer. That's how we met. I've got his picture around here somewhere.

> EVELYN *hands him a portrait of a handsome naval officer.*

EVELYN	Are you comfortable John?
JOHN	Oh yes.
EVELYN	I should put on something decent. You must be getting ideas.
JOHN	No, no!
EVELYN	Would you mind doing me up, John? Tell me about you.

> JOHN *fastens the button with great concentration.*

JOHN	There is not much to say. I am born in Russia, come to Canada in 1924. My family is Mennonite, you know. They work real hard all the time. I don't like that life so much so I come to work in Hamilton. My brother-in law, Jacob, he has some fruit farms and a cannery at Beamsville.

EVELYN	I was born in Grimsby!
JOHN	Is that so? (*smiling*) Just down the road.
EVELYN	Your family has a fruit farm and a cannery. You own part of that?
JOHN	Yes. (*hesitant*) I own some shares in that.
EVELYN	And you never married?
JOHN	No.
EVELYN	You're so nervous. That's kind of cute in a guy. Listen, I have to clean this place up.
JOHN	I help you. I like to do the chores (*taking his jacket off*).
EVELYN	(*amazed*) Jeez, I never knew a guy to do dishes before. Never.
JOHN	I like to pitch in. (*pause*) I like just to be around you.

> EVELYN *leans against* JOHN's *chest. He is surprised and thrilled.*

EVELYN	I bet you treat a girl real nice and gentle. You got any cigarettes, John?
JOHN	I'm sorry, I don't smoke. I will go and get some..
EVELYN	Never mind. We've got better things to do.

> *They kiss passionately.*

KEITH	The poor sap.
IRIS	He was in way over his head.

> JOHN *exits smiling blissfully.*
> EVELYN *glares at* ALEXANDRA.

ALEXANDRA	Who is this fellow, this foreigner?
EVELYN	His name is John. He's a hell of a nice guy.
ALEXANDRA	It's plain to see, he hasn't a penny to his name.

Change focus to WOOD *and* PRESTON - *interrogation.*

WOOD	Mrs. Dick, the man who drove the car, who had the sack with him, what did he look like?
EVELYN	Inclined to be stocky and dark featured. His hair was wavy like yours.
WOOD	Would you guess his nationality?
EVELYN	Italian.
WOOD	How was he dressed?
EVELYN	Black shoes.
WOOD	Black oxfords.
EVELYN	And a blue suit.
WOOD	A blue suit with stripes in it?
EVELYN	Yes.
WOOD	No cuff?
EVELYN	No cuff.
WOOD	Well-dressed then?

> WOOD *lights a match but before he can light his pipe* EVELYN *leans in to light her cigarette, leans back and exhales.*

EVELYN	Yes, with a heavy odour of shaving lotion or hair tonic.
WOOD	How did he talk?
EVELYN	He wasn't talking much to me.
WOOD	Did you conspire with him to murder your husband?
EVELYN	No, no.
WOOD	Mrs. Dick, did you take any actual part in the killing of your husband?
EVELYN	No no, I know nothing about where his legs, arms or hands are.
WOOD	But you do know they are missing?
EVELYN	Yes.

The torso bleeds, staining the shroud.

IRIS	So did most of the country by this time.
PRESTON	(*confidentially*) Inspector, should we put out a notice on this Italian fellow?
WOOD	(*deadpan*) I don't know, Clarence, she just gave a pretty good description of me. Get Probable Cause Warrants issued for 214 Rosslyn and 32 Carrick. Search them from top to bottom.

Change focus to KEITH *and* IRIS.

KEITH	Yes, the rickety wheels of fate's screwy scooter were clattering across the battered cobblestones of Justice.
IRIS	That phrase ought to impress the illiterati.

KEITH   If it makes you laugh, then good. You're the type
         would never shell out for *True Crime* anyway.
         You'd just sneak read it at the beauty parlour.

IRIS   Yes, when I'm in having my nails sharpened.

         ***Change focus** to interrogation.*

WOOD   Mrs. Dick, you knew of this terrible murder and
         you never saw fit to tell the authorities?

EVELYN   No, I am scared in case I get a bomb or
         something in my home. It's all right to talk but
         look at how those foreigners get back at you.
         Suppose they put a time bomb under my veranda
         or back porch, then where would I be?

         ***Change focus** to* IRIS *and* KEITH.

IRIS   I heard a rumour Evelyn was Rocco Perri's
         illegitimate daughter.

KEITH   (*vamping* to ALEXANDRA) Heey, mizza
         MacLean, you come onna my house, we far
         amore com passione! (*as* ALEXANDRA) Well,
         if you insist -- I'll give you three minutes,
         Mister Perri.

         ALEXANDRA glowers at KEITH.

         ***Change focus** to* WOOD *presenting*
         EVELYN *with a typed statement.*

EVELYN   What time will I be going home?

WOOD   You won't be going home. You will be held in
         custody for questioning.

IRIS   Not arrested, you notice; held in custody, detained
         for questioning.

WOOD   Will you sign this statement?

IRIS
: Legally, she could have walked out of the station but they didn't tell her that.

EVELYN
: Yes. (*pause*) I was just wondering if there was anything I overlooked to tell you.

> EVELYN *signs, as if it was a movie deal.*

> ***Change focus*** *to* IRIS *and* KEITH.

IRIS
: I've never seen a woman so anxious to please.

KEITH
: To please men. Everything in that woman's life came down to one basic desire.

IRIS
: (*mocking*) The intolerable urge. No, Evelyn was searching for love like any woman and she thought she'd found it in John Dick.

KEITH
: What are you smoking there, loco weed?

IRIS
: Did either of the parents show up for the wedding?

KEITH
: No. Donald didn't even know about it and Evelyn and her mother had had a huge quarrel.

> ***Change focus*** *to* EVELYN *and* ALEXANDRA.

EVELYN
: You might as well know, mother, we're getting married. We took out the licence.

ALEXANDRA
: What? Is this my reward for raising you, sending you to the best schools - you'll marry a motorman.

EVELYN
: Stay the hell out of my business!

ALEXANDRA
: You're too damned headstrong.

> *Change focus to* JOHN *and*
> EVELYN *exchanging vows.* KEITH
> *throws confetti on them.*

KEITH   They got married in the chapel at The Church of
the Ascension. (C. of E.) After, they went to the
Majestic Restaurant.

> KEITH *serves them coffee which*
> JOHN *spikes with a mickey from his*
> *coat. He leans over to kiss* EVELYN
> *but she puffs defiantly on her cigarette.*

EVELYN   I told mother about us. She's not too happy.

JOHN   Let me talk to her.

EVELYN   I don't think so.

JOHN   I saw a house today, for sale with Moore &
Davis.

EVELYN   Where?

JOHN   Barton & Emerald.

EVELYN   Down there with all the dagoes, are you crazy?

JOHN   It's a big house. Its got rooms we could rent out.

EVELYN   You want me to run a flophouse?

JOHN   No, I just thought to help to pay for the expense.
The down payment is pretty high. I...I know you
got some money...so maybe...(*faltering*)

EVELYN   (*bristling*) It's the husband's job to provide. You
got money in the bank and shares in the cannery.

JOHN   Yes, but not so much I am rich.

EVELYN   (*leaning across the table and lowering her voice*)
                  John, you are working in a gold mine. Why
                  come home with empty pockets every day?

                  JOHN *looks at her, totally confused.*

EVELYN   Do what the old man does, help yourself. He's
                  been skimming off fareboxes for years.

JOHN   (*stunned*) I could never steal. Never.

EVELYN   Well then, you have disappointed me. (*darkening*)
                  Call up your brother-in-law, he's loaded.
                  (*standing up*) You better think of something.

JOHN   Where are you going?

EVELYN   Home. My mother was right about you.

                  Change focus to KEITH *and* IRIS.

IRIS   She left him on their wedding night.

KEITH   Alexandra said Evelyn came to bed about
                  midnight.

IRIS   Why does a woman of twenty-four sleep with her
                  mother?

KEITH   It was a small apartment?

IRIS   They shared a bed at 32 Carrick and that's a three
                  bedroom house. When the family was at 214
                  Rosslyn, she and Alexandra slept in the same
                  bed, there, too.

KEITH   Yeah, Donald lived in the cellar with his guns,
                  his booze and his dog. Alexandra practically fed
                  him under the door.

IRIS   A neighbour told me he was partial to midnight
                  target practice.

> DONALD, *drunk, aims a handgun and fires.* **Change focus** *to interrogation at centre table.*

PRESTON   Well, how did you pass the night?

EVELYN   I slept okay but breakfast was lousy.

PRESTON   You just let me know if you're hungry.

> WOOD *'enters',* PRESTON *reacts defensively,* EVELYN *beams.*

EVELYN   Thank you Clarence, that'll be fine.

WOOD   Thank you, Sgt. Preston. (*to* EVELYN) We picked up your friend this morning?

EVELYN   Who's that?

WOOD   Bohozuk. Bill Bohozuk. Lives down on Picton Street? Drives a two-tone blue Buick Deluxe?

PRESTON   We found a slip of paper in John's room with the plate number on it.

EVELYN   What did Bill say?

WOOD   He denied having anything to do with this murder.

EVELYN   You know, Inspector, in what I told you yesterday, there were some things I left out or didn't get right.

> **Change focus** *to* IRIS *and* KEITH.

IRIS   Bill Bohozuk, oarsman extraordinaire.

KEITH   I always said he shoulda called his boat, The Hunky Dory.

IRIS   You would. How did she meet him?

KEITH   (*as* BILL) In the spring of 'forty-five. I was coming out of Bob's Grill at the corner of Barton & James. I noticed a black coupe stopped close beside my car. There was a dark girl behind the wheel. She smiled at me and I smiled back.

        EVELYN *scribbles on a piece of paper.*

KEITH   Hey lady, I can't get in my car.

EVELYN   Aren't you Bill Bohozuk?

KEITH   (*pleased*) Yeah.

EVELYN   I saw your picture in *The Spectator*.

KEITH   Uh-huh. What's your name?

EVELYN   Evelyn White. Get into the car, Bill.

        KEITH *mimes geting into the car as* BILL.

KEITH   (*recalling*) I met you at the track last year. Sportsman's Park?

EVELYN   You were with your wife.

KEITH   Oh Helen, well she's gone now.

EVELYN   Really, what happened?

KEITH   I came home one day and there she was -- gone.

EVELYN   You still row for Leander Boat Club?

KEITH   Soon as the ice melts, I'm out on the Bay.

EVELYN   You look in pretty good shape Bill.

KEITH   Same goes for you. That's a pretty flashy ring. Husband give you that?

EVELYN	Yes, before he was killed in the war.
KEITH	Geez, that's tough.
EVELYN	He was a Lt. Commander -- torpedoed in the North Sea.
KEITH	What ship?
EVELYN	*HMCS Wentworth*!

KEITH *as* BILL *puzzles over this.*

EVELYN	He left me pretty well-fixed though.
KEITH	Why don't we go for a beer?
EVELYN	I'd love to Bill but I'm looking at some houses for sale. Here's my number. You give me a call.

EVELYN *blows* BILL *a kiss.* KEITH *ceases to be* BILL.

IRIS	Why this urge to dally with a beefcake steelworker?
KEITH	Bill rowed for the Leander Boat Club. That's a big deal here. If you're an athlete in Hamilton, you got no problems getting lai---dates. Anyways Bill tried to call her a few times but she was never home. Finally he saw her again on King Street in late September of last year. (*as* BILL) We went to Haley's Hotel in Dundas for a few beers. After we made another date. I took her to a movie at the Tivoli Theatre on October 9th.
IRIS	Five days after she married John Dick?
KEITH	Bingo.

Change focus to JOHN *at door with* ALEXANDRA.

JOHN	Where she is?
ALEXANDRA	Evelyn has gone out.
JOHN	You say to me on phone, she is sick.
ALEXANDRA	A friend came and took her out.
JOHN	Why she has this fancy apartment? I am her husband. She should live with me!
ALEXANDRA	Her apartment is none of your business, Mr. Dick. How do you expect Evelyn to keep up with her social contacts if she doesn't have a nice apartment to entertain her friends in?
JOHN	You mean she is a social prostitute?
ALEXANDRA	No! She has rich friends and she has to have a nice place to entertain them.
JOHN	Can you lend me money for a down payment? Just a loan for a house. For Evelyn.
ALEXANDRA	You have no money of your own?
JOHN	Sure. I got some in the bank.
ALEXANDRA	What branch? (*as* JOHN *stutters*) Pahh! That is positive proof that you have nothing, not even a bankbook. You foreigners must have a lot of nerve, to come begging money of me.
JOHN	I may be foreigner but I am an honest man. I know where your money comes from.

> ALEXANDRA *exits, furious.* JOHN *waits for* EVELYN.
>
> ***Change focus*** *to* KEITH *as* BILL *walking with* EVELYN.

EVELYN	(*animated*) Gee, Bill, the movie was great.

KEITH   I seen better.

EVELYN   Isn't the first time...so special?

KEITH   (*bored*) I guess so.

EVELYN   Here we are.

KEITH   You got an apartment in Henson Park? Not bad.

EVELYN   Listen, Bill, I like you a lot. My husband left me pretty well off so if you ever need anything, give me a call.

> EVELYN *wants to be kissed but* JOHN *intrudes.*

JOHN   Listen you, Bohozuk. Get yourself another woman and stop bothering my wife.

KEITH   Hey, pal, I didn't know she was married. (*to* EVELYN) I don't like a liar. (*ceases being* BILL)

> ***Change focus*** *to* IRIS *at the map.*

KEITH   You'd think John would take a hint and take a hike.

IRIS   No, he was obsessed with her. Where is Henson Park Manor?

KEITH   In the southwest, right up James here. (*at the map*) It's a posh neighbourhood. Old money. Run the city.

IRIS   Why would Evelyn keep an apartment there?

KEITH   (*sly*) She had friends in the neighbourhood.

IRIS   Oh, there's Markland Street. I've chums from school who live there. David and Euphemia Holmes-Webster. Euphemia and I went to

IRIS	(*continued*) Havergal. David was at Upper Canada with my brother.
KEITH	Have you spoken to him lately?
IRIS	Yes, I thought we might all get together for a drink while I was here but he was very cool to the idea. David always thought me a touch outre. And becoming a reporter - well, not done.
KEITH	Websters are one of the Forty Families, part of the Under-The-Mountain Gang
IRIS	Who calls them that?
KEITH	Chums of mine in the North End.
IRIS	I see. Well I'm sure the Websters wouldn't appreciate having someone like Evelyn as a neighbour.
KEITH	Perhaps. A month later, she and her mother, moved to 32 Carrick.
IRIS	Who paid for that house?
KEITH	The deed was in Evelyn's name but the day they moved in, John was waiting for them.
	Change focus *to* ALEXANDRA, EVELYN *and* JOHN *confrontation.*
ALEXANDRA	How did you get in here?
JOHN	I got the key from the agent.
ALEXANDRA	Why on earth would he give you the key?
JOHN	I am the husband.
EVELYN	We don't want you here.

JOHN   Well, I am here to stay. You are my wife and
                this is my house.

EVELYN   (*shrugging*) Well, okay. Would you mind taking
                those boxes upstairs?

                Change focus *to* KEITH *and* IRIS.

KEITH   I figure she made up her mind right there to
                knock him off. He was causing her too much
                trouble.

IRIS   No, John told his landlady, Mrs. Kammerer, that
                he had a miserable life there because of
                Alexandra. (*German acccent*) "John never had a
                private talk with his wife without the mother
                interfering.

                Change focus *to* ALEXANDRA
                hovering over EVELYN *and* JOHN
                arguing.

JOHN   Why your mother put a padlock on the attic
                door? She should put one on her mouth.

EVELYN   To stop you snooping around.

JOHN   And those trunks and suitcases up there, they are
                locked. What is in them?

EVELYN   You wouldn't be interested. They're just my
                school things.

IRIS   (*surprised*) He knew about those suitcases?

EVELYN   Anyway, this is my house, not yours.

JOHN   I am your husband by law and I got certain
                rights.

EVELYN   My name is on the deed.

JOHN	I talk to the lawyer. He will put my name on that deed.
ALEXANDRA	(*to* EVELYN) Did you hear that? (*to* JOHN) You are such a miserable, dirty foreigner.
JOHN	I can show you in court for a liar and your Dad for a thief. I know you are whoring me with that Bohozuk.
EVELYN	Watch out, you've gotten Bill mad and he's in with the gangs in the bumping-off business.

Change focus to interrogation.

WOOD	So Bill and your husband were not on friendly terms.
EVELYN	Far from it. In February, Bill borrowed money from me.
WOOD	Why?
EVELYN	He was expecting a job to be done and he needed two hundred dollars.
WOOD	What kind of a job?
EVELYN	John to be fixed.
WOOD	Did you get it back?
EVELYN	I did. In tens and twenties.
WOOD	What did Bill say when he returned it?
EVELYN	He said, 'I am bringing back the money because the gang were too busy to take care of him just now'.

Change focus to KEITH and IRIS.

KEITH	She's just trying to make Bill the scapegoat.
IRIS	Bill could easily hire a killer for two hundred dollars. This is Hamilton, after all.
KEITH	You believe that gangster story?

Change focus to interrogation.

EVELYN	As I explained, I did not want to take the torso in the car but Romanelli threatened me with a nickel-plated revolver in one pocket and a scalping knife in the other that I would do as I was told or you-know-what would happen to me.
WOOD	Who is Romanelli?
EVELYN	The Italian, later I found, well, that he finished John. Driving along to get rid of the torso, Romanelli told me that himself and his mate had asked John how would he like they were going up to the top of the Mountain for a drink and so John went along with the other two, one being Romanelli and the other I don't know. They had a bottle of Jamaica Rum, gin and ginger ale and Dago red wine. They drove along the Mountain, stopping on the outskirts of Hannon where they opened the bottle of rum and later went on as far as Glanford and went down a quiet road there or a deserted road. John got suspicious of going way out there because he was due to go to work at 4:11. They got stuck and John said, "You have done this on purpose to keep me late. I won't come again with you wops". And with that, Romanelli let him have it. One shot in the back of the neck and one through the right eyeball.
WOOD	Were you in the car when this happened?
EVELYN	No.

WOOD	This conversation that you are telling me, that took place between you and Romanelli while you were driving along the Mountain with the torso?
EVELYN	Right. He had remarked that he was being paid by Bill Bohozuk to dispose of John. I understood it was on the installment plan. I'm tired now. Can I get something to eat?
WOOD	Fine. Sgt. Preston will see to it. (*to* PRESTON) Clarence, she's putting her head in the noose; give her whatever she wants.
IRIS	(*to* KEITH) You're a font of arcane information; How long does it take to dismember a body?

Change focus to PRESTON
explaining to WOOD.

PRESTON	Assuming a proper saw, like Donald's here, the Coroner estimated the legs, arms and head could be sawn off within a minimum of half an hour.

Change focus to KEITH *and* IRIS.

IRIS	By a woman?
KEITH	Somewhere out there were some bloody hands that needed a whole heap of washing.
IRIS	There's a clumsy metaphor; 'a heap of washing' suggests a load of laundry not Pontius Pilate.
KEITH	You know what I mean; 'Bloody hands' as in - Whoever cut up the body?

Change focus to DONALD *grabbing*
EDDIE.

DONALD	Eddie, ma wee pet's in terrible trouble. It's her fault, bitch I married. Her fault. Gie me a ride over to Carrick Street.

> DONALD *picks up a heavy burlap*
> *sack, (the head?) and crosses to*
> ALEXANDRA *who lets him pass out*
> *the door and then fans herself.*

KEITH   He did it to protect his daughter.

IRIS   Or to cover his tracks.

KEITH   You think she's Miss Innocence?

> ***Change focus*** *to* PRESTON *and*
> EVELYN.

EVELYN   Why, hello Clarence.

PRESTON   Mrs. Dick, your husband's funeral will be held today. Do you wish to attend?

EVELYN   No, thank you.

PRESTON   The Press will want to know why. What should I tell them?

EVELYN   Tell them I have The Curse. I've used three pads already today.

> ***Change focus*** *to* KEITH *and* IRIS.

KEITH   Christ, did we howl at that one.

IRIS   No doubt. Something in the Hamilton air fosters a morbid sense of humour. I remember taking a walk one day and came upon children, skipping.

KEITH   Oh, yeah, I know it! (*skipping*)

> She cut off his arms!
> She cut off his legs!
> She cut off his head!
> Ohh! How could you Mrs. Dick?
> How could you miss-his-dick?

KEITH   Get it?

                   IRIS *deadpans.*

                   Change focus *to interrogation as*
                   PRESTON *takes notes.*

WOOD   March 22nd, 1946, Mrs.. Evelyn G. Dick of the
                   City of Hamilton. You are charged with
                   vagrancy.

IRIS   Vagrancy! Wood was more a vagrant than she.

KEITH   It's just a holding charge - a normal police
                   practice.

                   Change focus *to* IRIS *and* KEITH.

IRIS   And is it a normal police practice to prevent a
                   lawyer from seeing his client? At this very
                   moment a John Evans arrived at the Station.
                   Donald had retained him on Evelyn's behalf. He
                   went to the Detective's Office;
                   (*as* EVANS) Sgt. Preston, I'd like to see my
                   client.

PRESTON   And who might that be Mr. Evans?

IRIS   Mrs. Evelyn Dick.

PRESTON   Why, she's down at the Jail.

IRIS   I phoned the Governor and he said she was taken
                   away hours ago. Where is she?

PRESTON   Have a look in the Duty Room.

                   As EVANS *turns away* PRESTON
                   chuckles. Change focus to WOOD *with
                   tickets and watch chain.*

WOOD   Mrs. Dick, this watch has been identified as John
                Dick's. The serial numbers on these tickets
                correspond to those issued to him on the
                morning of March sixth. We found these in your
                bedroom drawer. This is your husband's
                conductor's punch. It was in the pocket of your
                mother's sealskin coat.

ALEXANDRA   We share that coat, both of us wear it, Inspector.

WOOD   How do these come to be in your house?

EVELYN   March sixth, I got a telephone call from Bill
                Bohozuk and he said, "We've got him at last,"
                and he told me to meet him at The Royal
                Connaught right away. I went and was met there
                by Romanelli who gave me those and a small tin
                box with some more tickets. He said, "Here's
                some stuff that Bill thought you would like to
                have. Then I went home and later Romanelli
                brought the car into the back lane. I remarked
                that there was a lot of blood on the car and he
                said, "That will come off alright". There was a
                blanket in the back of the car and it was covered
                with blood. Wrapped up in a piece of cloth was a
                part of the face, which was all smashed, and
                some other parts which he said they had tried to
                burn and were not able to succeed in. I went in
                the house and told my Mother that John had been
                fixed. She asked me, "Is there anything out
                there?" I told her there was a couple of pieces left
                over. Pieces of flesh and skin, I burned in the
                furnace later.

                Change focus to PRESTON *and*
                EVANS.

IRIS   (*as* EVANS) She's not there, Sergeant. You're
                questioning her, aren't you?

PRESTON   No. She's been sent back to the Jail.

IRIS
You're not going to shuffle me off to Buffalo, Preston. I demand to see Mrs. Dick.

PRESTON
Cool your heels, little man. (*gesturing with papers*)

IRIS
What the hell have you got there? That's a statement. (*trying to get by*) This is illegal, godammit! I insist upon seeing my client.

> ***Change focus*** *to* EVANS *bursting in on interrogation.*

IRIS
(*as* EVANS, *to* WOOD) You're not to speak to her again without my knowledge and permission. Mrs. Dick, keep your mouth shut and bloody well shut if you know what shut means. (*ceases to be* EVANS)

KEITH
She liked that line. She used it herself two days later.

IRIS
Yes, when they finally got around to charging her with murder.

WOOD
Now, Mrs. Dick, there is an information against you charging that you did on or about the 6th day of March 1946 at the City of Hamilton or in the County of Wentworth unlawfully murder...

EVELYN
Murder!

WOOD
...John Dick contrary to the provisions of Section 259 and 263 of the Criminal Code. Now do you wish to say anything in relation to that charge?

EVELYN
Well, I know that I did not.

WOOD
Now you have given us three statements, do you remember the contents of them?

EVELYN
Well, yes.

WOOD	Are they true or false?
EVELYN	Just one.
WOOD	Do you wish to change any part of them?
EVELYN	Change the first two.
WOOD	You want to change the first two, and the last statement I take it then, is true so far as you went before we were interrupted.?
EVELYN	It is.
WOOD	Do you want to go on from there?
EVELYN	I can't. I am told to keep my mouth shut and bloody well shut if I know what shut means.
WOOD	In view of this charge of murder now being laid against you, you still want to remain silent?
EVELYN	Yes, I am told to.
WOOD	Very good, I guess that is the end of the interview.
EVELYN	Will that be laid against Bill too?
KEITH	She's always trying to implicate Bill Bohozuk.
IRIS	Why not, he's got a motive and a gun?
KEITH	Bill's gun was never fired. Donald's was...

Change focus: PRESTON *with gun.*

PRESTON	One nickelplated, Harrington and Richardson calibre .32 revolver, serial number 734. It was in a gun cabinet in the home of Donald MacLean at 214 Rosslyn St. The bore has traces of black powder, evidence of recent discharge.

WOOD	How recent?
PRESTON	Within days, or possibly weeks.
WOOD	Black powder. What about this? (*picking up ammunition*)
PRESTON	Dominion .32 calibre ammunition, black powder type, cartridges of an old make. It's all smokeless powder now, has been since the Great War.
WOOD	So if you fire these inside a car, you get..?
PRESTON	...smoke. And plenty of it.
IRIS	Why wait so long to charge the parents?

> ***Change focus*** *to* WOOD *and* PRESTON.

WOOD	We need more proof. Time to tighten the screws on the old folks. That'll get her talking again.

> PRESTON *approaches* DONALD *and* ALEXANDRA.

PRESTON	I have here a warrant for your arrest. You are jointly charged with the murder of John Dick.

> ALEXANDRA *swoons.*

PRESTON	Donald, d'you wish to make a statement?
DONALD	(*defiant*) I'll say nothin' to nobody.
ALEXANDRA	I'd have a word with you, Inspector. In private.

> ***Change focus*** *to* PRESTON *and* EVELYN *at the jail.*

EVELYN	Clarence, I sent a message for you on Wednesday; why didn't you come down to the Jail?

PRESTON	I was out of town, didn't get the note until late last night. What's on your mind?
EVELYN	The old man, he's in on it.
PRESTON	Who do you mean?
EVELYN	My father. He loaned Bohozuk his gun.
PRESTON	How do you know?
EVELYN	I saw it. You've got to help me. I am not going to be left holding the bag.

> EVELYN *and* PRESTON *move to the*
> *interrogation table and* WOOD *'enters'.*

WOOD	Is Bohozuk in this thing?
EVELYN	Absolutely. Will it make it any worse for me if I tell everything?
WOOD	I cannot answer that question. You are putting me on the spot. If you want to talk, I will listen.

> WOOD *motions for* PRESTON *to*
> *record the conversation.*

EVELYN	My father hated John Dick's guts. Then John found out about him stealing, and things went from bad to worse. My father paid Bohozuk three or four hundred dollars to do the job, and he was sitting in the Balmoral Hotel getting drunk whilst it was being done.
IRIS	Three or four hundred dollars was pocket money for Donald.
WOOD	Let's go back to Wednesday, March the 6th.
IRIS	Ash Wednesday. Symbolic of mortality.

EVELYN	I met John near the Astor around two p.m. and then went to The King George, but couldn't get a drink, as it was closing time.
KEITH	Closing time. Symbolic of Ontario.
EVELYN	Then we met Bohozuk, and we drove over the mountain.
WOOD	Who was driving?
EVELYN	I was and Bohozuk some of the time.
WOOD	So you were there?
EVELYN	If I say yes, will it be worse for me?
WOOD	I'm not answering that, I can't say. How many shots were fired?
EVELYN	Three. (*counting on her fingers*) How many bullets in my father's gun? How many will it hold?

> EVELYN *looks to* PRESTON. WOOD *signals him not to respond.*

EVELYN	Five, I think. There was one chamber empty.
WOOD	Were you in a barn?
EVELYN	No, on a sideroad.
WOOD	This happened on a sideroad in daylight?
EVELYN	Sure.
PRESTON	What if you were asked to take a little car ride and show us the spot where it happened?
EVELYN	Would it help me?
PRESTON	It would certainly back up your story.

> EVELYN *ponders this.*

IRIS   So, did they inform her lawyer about this proposition?

KEITH   Wood asked the Crown Attorney and was told it was perfectly legal.

EVELYN   Sure I'll go. Say, I'm hungry.

PRESTON   (*handing her two chocolate bars.*) Here.

> ***Change focus*** *to* KEITH *and* IRIS *setting up 'car' with four chairs.*

KEITH   So they took a drive in the country. Evelyn went along happily.

IRIS   It was a nice sunny day. She just wanted to get out of jail for a few hours. Who sat where?

KEITH   Wood drove the car and Preston rode in the back beside her. She's here right behind Wood.

> WOOD *drives.* EVELYN *is in the rear, behind* WOOD. PRESTON *is to her right.* IRIS *and* KEITH *trace the route on the map.*

EVELYN   Oh, what a glorious day! Can we stop and pick up some movie magazines and some love stories?

WOOD   I'm afraid not. Which way now?

EVELYN   Well get out to 53 Highway by DeGeer's Hotel.

KEITH   (*at map*) The intersection of Gage Avenue and 53 Highway.

EVELYN   There is DeGeer's. Turn left. Turn right up the
          stone road, south. Look for a farmhouse, it is
          vacant, it is a white house, with a blue roof.
          There is the farm.

WOOD   It hasn't got a blue roof.

EVELYN   No, my mistake. It was blue trim.

WOOD   What happened here?

EVELYN   Nothing but now that I see the house I know
          where I am, I can direct you from here. Turn
          around. I was driving, John was sitting on my
          right, and Bill Bohozuk was in the back seat,
          alone. Turn right. Here is about where John
          started to get drunk. Both John and Bill had been
          drinking while we were driving, but I was only
          drinking ginger ale. Drive on. Turn left. Turn
          right. At this point John was worrying about
          being late for work. He had to be back on the job
          somewhere around four o'clock, and he wanted to
          turn north towards Hamilton. I saw Bill in the
          rear-view mirror, he was waving his hand like
          this, (*demonstrating*) in a "go ahead motion".
          Bohozuk said, "This is a shortcut back to the
          city, John." Turn right here.

          This road was a mess -- mud and water. The
          wipers were going, we had an awful job keeping
          the road. When we turned this corner John got
          mad and he said, "I can see it all now it's a plan.
          Tomorrow I am going to the lawyer to start
          divorce proceedings and name you as
          correspondent and instead of you being a big shot
          you will be the laughing stock of the men down
          at the plant." The argument got hotter, until we
          came to a spot where there were double telegraph
          poles. This is it right here. Stop. This is where
          Bohozuk shot John in the neck. (*placing her
          fingers on* WOOD's *neck at the hair line*) He
          shot John in the neck and blood spurted out of

EVELYN   (*continued*) the right eye. And the blood splashed
                    all over me. He shot him again right there,
                    through the head. (*placing her finger again*) I was
                    choking. The car was full, filled with gunpowder
                    smoke and I was covered with blood. I stopped
                    the car and got out the door and I got sick. I tried
                    to clean the blood off me. Bohozuk got out the
                    right hand door and pulled the blanket from the
                    seat and wrapped it over John's head. John
                    groaned so Bill said, "I'll finish him off." and
                    shot him in the chest.

WOOD   Is that true?

EVELYN   Yes.

WOOD   That doesn't add up.

EVELYN   What do you mean?

WOOD   I think you are lying.

                        WOOD *walks away.* EVELYN *and*
                        PRESTON *confer silently.*

IRIS   Why did he say that?

KEITH   Because there were two gunshot wounds in the
                    chest, three and a half inches apart.

                        KEITH *'gets' in* JOHN's *seat.* JOHN
                        watches not indicating truth or untruth.

KEITH   The bullet went in here and out here. It didn't
                    even go through the ribs. But she said Bohozuk
                    shot him the other way around.

                        WOOD *returns to the 'car'.* EVELYN
                        stands to meet him.

EVELYN   You misunderstood me Inspector. You are too
                  hasty. I am not lying, I am telling the truth, and
                  I am not going to be left holding the bag for
                  anybody.

WOOD   Well, tell me what happened.

EVELYN   (*getting behind the wheel*) I was here. Bohozuk
                  fired the two shots, and blood splashed all over
                  me and everything, and the gunpowder smoke
                  was so bad I nearly choked. I stopped the car, I
                  got out; (*getting out*) John was slumped forward.
                  The Indian blanket was right across the seat; I
                  had been sitting on part of it. Bohozuk came
                  around and pulled the blanket out from where I
                  had been sitting and covered John with it.
                  Bohozuk then got behind the wheel. Then John
                  groaned. So Bill turned like this...(*turning half
                  right*) pulled the gun out of his hip pocket, and
                  said, "I had better finish him off" and shot John I
                  thought in the stomach or chest. He drove to the
                  garage at Carrick Street and John Dick's body
                  was placed in the garage by Bohozuk. Then we
                  drove up town to The Royal Connaught Hotel
                  where I let him off. Then I drove back home,
                  stopping at a drug store to buy some *It* cleaning
                  fluid. I tried to clean some of the blood off my
                  blouse and my stockings. I took the blanket
                  home and washed it. (*yawning*) Say could we
                  stop at the Majestic Restaurant for supper? I'd
                  kill for a chicken dinner.

                          Change focus *to* IRIS *and* KEITH *as*
                          they 'strike' the 'car'.

IRIS   What a vivid imagination.

KEITH   No, a good eye for detail; the smoke, the blood
                  gushing out. She was there.

IRIS   Perhaps, but it doesn't mean she pulled the trigger. Besides, if the bullet went through his eye, why didn't it hit the windshield?

Change focus to interrogation.

WOOD   When did you next see the body?

EVELYN   In the garage on the Thursday evening.

WOOD   That's March 7th. In what condition?

EVELYN   The legs and arms were gone but the head was still there but not quite cut from the body.

WOOD   That doesn't add up either.

EVELYN   What do you mean?

WOOD   It means, I don't believe you.

EVELYN   Well, it's the truth.

WOOD   Mrs. Dick, it's only fair to tell you that we have in our possession the blue, striped Arrow shirt which John Dick wore the day he went missing. (*presenting the shirt*) It was found early the next morning, March the 7th, on the mountainside road. The arms are cut off, it's saturated with blood. It is buttoned up the front completely, including the collar. I don't believe it would be possible to get that shirt off a body while the head was attached. (*no response*) Do you have anything else to say?

EVELYN   No.

WOOD   Alright, that is your story. Whatever you're telling me today is voluntary. You sent for us. Previously you involved a man named Romanelli in this murder. Is he in the picture?

EVELYN   No -- well, there is probably a Romanelli, but he is not in this case. Anyway, my lawyer told me I don't have to say anything.

WOOD   Very good then, I will go.

EVELYN   Bye now.

> *Change focus to* WOOD, PRESTON *and* ALEXANDRA *in interrogation.*

WOOD   Mrs. MacLean, you have told us that at six p.m. on the day of the murder of John Dick, your daughter tried to put the Packard into the Carrick garage.

ALEXANDRA   Yes, she was trying a few times and I said she might know that large car wouldn't fit in that garage. I got annoyed at her and told her to get that car off the place, altogether. She told me to mind my own business. Then she backed the car up the alleyway.

WOOD   When did you see her again?

ALEXANDRA   Eight or nine o'clock that night.

PRESTON   Tell the Inspector about Friday March the eighth.

ALEXANDRA   Friday, March the eighth, Evelyn suggested I take a walk in the afternoon with wee Heather. It was a beautiful sunny day. We went up as far as Sherman and around that way, so I knew it was about time for John Dick's car to come along -- he always sounded the bell or the gong for Heather and she would wave her hand -- so I saw his streetcar but instead I saw another man driving. So I went home and I said to Evelyn, "John was not in his car today." She said, "Well, it is not likely he will trouble me again, and you will never see him on a car." I said "Why, there is nothing happened to him, he's not been killed?"

ALEXANDRA   (*continued*) Her face flushed, and the way she said it gave me the impression that something serious had happened. She said, "Yes, John Dick is dead, and you keep your mouth shut."

WOOD   And you'll swear to all this in court?

ALEXANDRA   Aye.

> *Change focus to* EVELYN *standing to face the jury.*

IRIS   Evelyn faced that jury with not whit of fear, no emotion at all. She knew what was coming. The judge hadn't allowed a single defence motion or objection in the entire trial. Remember his charge to the men of the jury? (*as the judge* "Are the facts of this case consistent with any other rational conclusion but that the accused is guilty. Personally I do not think so".

> *Change focus to* KEITH *with* WOOD *and* PRESTON *outside court.*

KEITH   A few questions, Inspector?

> PRESTON *bristles but* WOOD *is magnanimous.*

WOOD   Go ahead, son.

KEITH   How long you figure the jury will be out?

WOOD   As long as justice takes.

KEITH   What are your chances?

PRESTON   (*guffawing*) A lot better than hers.

WOOD   Son, I've got nothing at stake here. Those twelve men, good and true, it's their's to decide.

KEITH   Would it bother you to see a woman hanged?

WOOD   My job is finished. I bear no ill will against
                 Mrs. Dick.

PRESTON   She's a lovely lass but she'll be none the worse
                 for a bit of hanging.

>   ***Change focus*** *to verdict and sentence.*

IRIS   (*as clerk*) Has the jury reached a verdict?

KEITH   (*as jury foreman*) We find the accused guilty of
                 murder, your Lordship. Guilty with a
                 recommendation of mercy.

>   WOOD *and* PRESTON *shake hands.*
>   KEITH *takes a flash photo.*

IRIS   (*as judge*) Evelyn Dick, stand up. Have you
                 anything to say why sentence should not be
                 passed upon you?

EVELYN   I want my case appealed.

IRIS   (*as judge*) Evelyn Dick, the sentence of this court
                 is that you be brought from here to the place
                 whence you came and there be kept in close
                 confinement till the 7th day of January in the
                 year 1947 and upon that day you be taken to the
                 place of execution and that there you be hanged
                 by the neck until dead. May God have mercy on
                 your soul. The jury's recommendation for mercy
                 will be forwarded to the proper authorities.

>   *Lights down on* EVELYN *at centre*
>   *stage.*

>   *End of Act One.*

HOW COULD YOU, MRS. DICK?

Act Two

The Mug Shot - Hamilton Police Dept.

ACT TWO

IRIS

Lights up on cast in same positions as at the end of Act One.

It was the moment I heard the guilty verdict that I began to believe in her innocence.

KEITH

You're kidding.

IRIS

No.

KEITH

You'd've been the only one, that night.

PRESTON *takes* EVELYN *into custody. Tense, threatening music under crowd sounds.*

IRIS

That's right. Outside the courthouse, the nightly witch hunt was about to begin. They gathered in the darkening gloom, a horrifying, faceless mob, driven to a frenzy by jealousy and the desire for revenge. Evelyn's immorality outraged the Christian faithful and now she must die. But for every hypocrite who condemned her, there were two bobbysoxers keeping scrapbooks.

KEITH

Don't believe everything you write in the papers. (*reading his own story*) News of the verdict raced through the crowd like destiny's red rocket. They were going to hang Evelyn Dick by the neck till stone cold dead. When she came out onto the granite stairway, the crowd surged and she cried out, breathlessly. (*over a deafening roar from the crowd*)

KEITH   (*continued*) Her eyes widened in fear and she stiffened like a deer on the highway, frozen in the headlights.

                            PRESTON *lights a match.* EVELYN *smokes with a shaky hand.*

IRIS   It was a brave show but she was frightened of the mob. They were pushing and shoving, trampling each other to get to her. It was a sick, sordid scene.

KEITH   Ooh, alliteration! Sick, sordid scene. It was great. You could see pinpoints of light, cigarette ends glowing in the dark; flash powder and smoke, blinding light and the newsreel cameras grinding away. Kids ran about, screaming. The cops bulled their way through the crowd, surrounding her like bodyguards. As the big black taxi inched through the gawking hordes, she'd wave to them. It was a movie and Evelyn was the star.

                            EVELYN *waves to the crowd.*

IRIS   But you never knew which role she would play; Scarlet Woman, Grieving Widow, Elegant Lady. Anyone but the janitor's dark-eyed daughter. In their eyes, I suppose, she had lived like a star, glamorous, carefree and rich.

KEITH   It was the sex that drew the crowds! Not that 'within the bounds of holy matrimony' stuff. Real sex, furtive, forbidden, tantalizing, like everybody secretly craves.

IRIS   In your case, it's no secret. Yes, sex, but many of those women saw Evelyn's promiscuity as defiance.

KEITH   She was a nymphomaniac — no man alive could satisfy her.

IRIS   Nonsense! Evelyn wanted love because she'd
                      grown up in a home where there was none.

KEITH   Hey, Donald and Alexandra hated each other but
                      they loved their daughter. On the night she was
                      condemned...

                      Change focus to DONALD, *in cuffs,
                      grabbing* KEITH's *sleeve in a flashback.*

DONALD   Have you seen ma Evelyn? How's she takin' it?

KEITH   As well as could be expected, Donald.

DONALD   Oh, aye. Aye. It's a terrible thing, hanging a
                      woman. Did her send any word to me?

KEITH   No, Donald.

                      Change focus to IRIS *and* KEITH.

IRIS   He was feeling guilty because Evelyn was going
                      to hang in his place.

KEITH   Donald was only in jail because he tried to help
                      her like any father would. Look at the old lady --
                      she doted on Evelyn.

IRIS   Really? I interviewed Alexandra the very night
                      Evelyn was condemned. The house was claustro-
                      phobic, a miniature Victorian home but the
                      rooms were too small, the furniture far too large
                      and grand. Everything was immaculate and
                      suffocating. There was a beautiful silver dish on
                      the coffee table and I couldn't help admiring it.

                      Change focus to ALEXANDRA.

ALEXANDRA   That has been in my family for years. I brought
                      it with me from Scotland.

IRIS   (*to* KEITH) But I know my silver. That dish was
                      made in Niagara Falls, two years ago.

ALEXANDRA	I've had wee Heather pray tonight to a picture of her mother.
IRIS	(*to* KEITH) I could hear her, the little girl, upstairs, crying for her mother.
ALEXANDRA	I can't stop thinking of Evelyn. She's shielding someone, Miss Muirson. Why doesn't she tell us who it was? I did not let my daughter down at her trial. I only told the truth as I was sworn to do. I want people to know that. (*sniffling*) Evelyn was a good girl. She loved housework from childhood up. She was the most wonderful housekeeper I ever knew, she'd clean and scrub and love it. She was scrubbing the stairs, the day the police...came for her.

The furnace clangs shut 'downstairs'.
IRIS *is startled.*

ALEXANDRA	That's the handyman cleaning the furnace. He keeps the furnace better than Evelyn did, although Evelyn was a good worker. (*peering at* IRIS' *notes*) Some people say that my husband paid for Evelyn to attend Loreto Academy. It was my mother's doing. She suggested that Evelyn attend a private school and when I wrote her that this was not feasible financially, she wrote from Scotland, "Think nothing of it" and sent a cheque. My family was very comfortably well off and we received excellent educations. I worked as a governess at Balmoral Castle. Evelyn's godmother is from a titled English family.
IRIS	I understand your daughter was very generous with her friends.
ALEXANDRA	My daughter was, of course, part of the younger social set, but Evelyn did not have sufficient money to enable her to entertain lavishly at The Brant Inn and bestow gifts as some people have been putting in the magazines. Furthermore, Evelyn was no friend of Rocco Perri.

                                    Change focus to KEITH *and* IRIS.

KEITH (*mimicing* ALEXANDRA) Titled English family, Balmoral Castle. Christ, what a snob. She wanted to climb into society and used her daughter's body for a ladder.

IRIS Bingo!

KEITH Why didn't you write that?

IRIS I did — subtly — between-the-lines — to get it past the editors. (*from notes*) There can be felt no more biting hurt than that of a young girl trapped between the o'erweening ambition of her mother and the social realities of a cold city. Rebuffed in trying to climb socially, she had made compromises. The kind of compromises which could only be regretted, never recalled. (*end of article*)

KEITH Evelyn's mother was pushing her into a world she didn't really like. She got her jollies at the track, boozing, the movies, football, screwing.

IRIS All the things that make Hamilton great.

                                    Change focus to ALEXANDRA *coming to* DONALD'*s table where he has made stacks of coins which she expertly rolls.*

KEITH And Mommy couldn't admit all her money came in nickels and dimes stolen by the drunkard of the Balmoral Tavern.

IRIS Surely that was just part of her income.

KEITH No. Over twenty years, Donald stole up to a quarter of a million dollars. (*shocking* IRIS) Best legit dough he ever made was two grand a year. Seventy-two cents an hour. Evelyn spent twenty-two hundred bucks in one year, just at Birks!

KEITH   (*continued*) Lots of guys are carrying around silver cigarette cases thanks to her. This one buddy of mine -- met her in a clothing store. Next day they deliver a tailored suit to his house - her treat. Evelyn spent money like water, even as a kid. The MacLeans had about fifty grand in joint accounts, two houses, a brand new Buick -- Evelyn had ten thou of her own. Donald had keys to the money-sorting room and the fareboxes.

> KEITH *pulls up* DONALD's *keychain, then a slip of paper.*

KEITH   Plus the combination to the company vault.

IRIS   You could say Donald was riding the golden streetcar.

KEITH   Yes, I could. (*scribbling it down*) But there are people that money can't buy.

> ***Change focus*** *to* PRESTON *and* DONALD.

PRESTON   Donald.

DONALD   This is a terrible business, Clarence.

PRESTON   Yes, Don. A fellow's dead. I've got a warrant here to search the house.

> PRESTON *retrieves a pair of black Oxford shoes.*

PRESTON   Whose shoes are these, Donald?

DONALD   They're mine. I use them for taking out the ashes.

PRESTON   (*examining shoes*) This looks like blood, Donald.

DONALD   If that's blood then they're no mine.

PRESTON	Do you know anything about the killing of John Dick?
DONALD	I know nothing about the killing of John Dick. I had nothing to do with it. Clarence, you come by tonight and there'll be ten thousand dollars in cash in the glove box of the Buick. Drive it away and nobody will ever know. Forget all about this.
PRESTON	Don, I'll pretend I didn't hear that. I've got a job to do and I'm here to do it. Empty your pockets.
	DONALD *empties coins from his denim smock onto the table.and some spill on the floor.*
IRIS	Why wasn't this bribe attempt brought up in Court?
KEITH	Maybe the cops figured the old drunk was already in enough trouble.
PRESTON	He had $884.00 cash in his pockets, $174.00 in change. We can't begin to count the number of streetcar tickets we've found. There was $4400.00 in 10's and 20's in the gun cabinet.
WOOD	How did he get away with this?
PRESTON	Don had the run of the HSR offices, he could come and go as he pleased. He was known to spend many hours there after quitting time.
	Change focus to IRIS *and* KEITH.
IRIS	John must have known of the thefts long before he was killed. Why didn't he tell the police?
KEITH	Maybe he was trying to blackmail Donald.
IRIS	But not for money -- for something both of them wanted --

KEITH & IRIS	(*together*) His daughter.
	Change focus *to* DONALD *and* JOHN *arguing violently.*
DONALD	You damn Russki, leave my daughter alone. You're tryin' to break up my home.
JOHN	She is my wife. I got licence. She better live with me or I take her to Court and whole town will know what a thief you are...
DONALD	You stay away from her you Polack or I will fix you forever.
JOHN	I can put you in the soup.
	DONALD *strikes* JOHN *who tries to fend him off.*
JOHN	I don't want to hit you, old man.
DONALD	I'll kill you. I'll blow your brains out.
	JOHN *turns away from* DONALD, *frightened by the intensity of the threat.*
	Change focus *to* KEITH *and* IRIS.
IRIS	You see, Donald was capable of murder. They almost hung an innocent woman.
KEITH	Hardly innocent. Thanks to the appeal I lost a great headline. Hamilton Harlot Hanged For Hacking Hubby Headless.
IRIS	Gorgeous Gal Gasps Gallows Goodbye.
KEITH	Scarlet Swinger Sez "I'm Dancing on Air with Hamilton Hemp!"

IRIS	You take a remarkably infantile pleasure in the ghoulish. It's almost endearing.
KEITH	Any of that Scotch left?
IRIS	Help yourself, I carry a spare. (*pouring drinks*) I'm sorry such an outmoded concept as justice interfered with your ecstatic prose but she deserved a fair trial.
KEITH	She had a fair trial.
IRIS	Nonsense. They used a trifling charge like vagrancy to hold her when they were questioning her about a murder. Why do you think J.J. Robinette took on her appeal? For the money? Robinette knew that she had been deprived of the basic protection any accused is entitled to under British law - and the Court of Appeal confirmed that by ordering the second trial.

Change focus to WOOD *and* PRESTON *in office.*

WOOD	You know what this decision means Clarence?
PRESTON	Yes. I think so.
WOOD	It means that all this paper, every statement she gave us is worthless. We've got to do the whole damn thing all over again. This time Robinette will make damn sure she won't talk.
PRESTON	What did we do wrong?
WOOD	We played by the rules but now the Court's changed them. Buck up, Clarence, we're not beat yet. It's just Round Two.

Change focus to KEITH *and* IRIS.

KEITH	Skip the legal mumbo-jumbo and those statements are pretty incriminating.

IRIS	She never says in any of them that she killed John, or that she arranged to have him killed. In number one it was Romanelli, in numbers two and three it was Romanelli killing John for Bill Bohozuk. On the car ride, it was Bohozuk committing the murder for Donald. How does Bohozuk account for himself on the day of the murder?

> **Change focus** *to* BILL BOHOZUK
> *interrogation.*

KEITH	(*as* BILL) In the morning I slept till noon then I went uptown to the beer parlour at The Connaught and met up with a couple of friends, Doug Hart and Clyde Zairtz. When the beverage room closed at 2 p.m., me and Hart went to see a movie at the Capitol. *The Dalton Boys* I think it was. After we returned to the beverage room and met two girls, Madeleine Dale and Pauline Folks. We spent the rest of the night drinking, so about ten o'clock, I scratched work and went to bed.
PRESTON	Most of this checks out Bill, but I looked in *The Spectator*. *The Dalton Boys* was not playing at The Capitol on the 6th of March.
KEITH	(*as* BILL) No?
PRESTON	No. Do you have any other explanation for your movements between 2 and 4 in the afternoon?
KEITH	No. I must have made a mistake. I thought I went to the show with one of the boys.
PRESTON	Why did you get two hundred dollars from Mrs. Dick?
KEITH	I borrowed it to fix my car. Listen, this is a railroad job. Give me truth serum, a lie detector, anything.

PRESTON	You're up shit creek, Bill, without your oar this time.
KEITH	I had nothing to do with this. (*ceases to be* BILL)

Change focus to KEITH *and* IRIS.

IRIS	So, where was Bohozuk between the hours of two and four? John Dick left The Windsor Hotel coffee shop to meet Evelyn about two.
KEITH	But Bill's Buick tested clean for blood and gunpowder. Besides, John wouldn't get into the car if Evelyn was with Bohozuk.
IRIS	What if she and John were parked in the country, drinking and Bohozuk drove out there in his own car, with the gun? He could shoot Dick and be back in his beer parlour in less than two hours.
KEITH	Bohozuk's gun hadn't been fired.
IRIS	He could have used Donald's gun like she said.
KEITH	Then why wouldn't Bill finish the job? Why leave her alone with the body? She couldn't possibly lift it out of the Packard on her own.
IRIS	Maybe that's where Donald took over. In any event, Donald had the motive, the opportunity and the weapon.

Change focus to WOOD *and* PRESTON *in office.*

WOOD	What were Donald's movements on March the sixth?
PRESTON	He was signed in as present all day at work but he could get away for hours at a time without being noticed. We can find no evidence of his movements the day of the murder.

WOOD	Alright. (*reading label on vial*) One fired .32 caliber lead bullet.
PRESTON	Found on the floor of the garage at Carrick St.
WOOD	Was it fired from Donald's gun?
PRESTON	Can't tell. The bullet is too damaged but microscopic examination shows four small white fragments on the bullet; bone matter but not conclusively human bone.
WOOD	It's unlikely the gun was fired in that garage.
PRESTON	It could have fallen out somehow, when the body parts were brought over to be burned. In this basket, maybe?

> WOOD *and* PRESTON *examine a blood-stained bushel basket with the logo: PEACOCK MEATS.*

WOOD	What about these stains?
PRESTON	Human blood, Type O, the same as John Dick.

> ***Change focus*** *to* ALEXANDRA *being interrogated.*

WOOD	Did your husband have any revolvers?
ALEXANDRA	Yes.
WOOD	Did he have ammunition?
ALEXANDRA	Yes. In a dresser drawer, full.
WOOD	In the cellar of 214 Rosslyn, were there any knives?
ALEXANDRA	Yes. One he used to cut meat for his dog.

>DONALD *is cutting chunks of meat and throwing it into a dog bowl.*

WOOD   How would you describe the knife?

ALEXANDRA   (*demonstrating size*) Just like a butcher's knife.

WOOD   And a number of saws?

ALEXANDRA   Yes.

>***Change focus*** *to* IRIS *giving a transcript to* KEITH.

IRIS   Raymond Castle was Superintendent of the Street Railway. Donald was always after him.

DONALD   Sir, check that damn Russian's bond money. He's short. Ma daughter's always havin' to gie him money.

KEITH   (*as* CASTLE) I've told you before, leave that to me, Donald.

>ALEXANDRA *surreptitiously removes money from* JOHN's *HSR satchel.* JOHN *'enters'* CASTLE's *office.*

KEITH   Whatever the problem between you and Donald, it's had a deleterious effect on your work habits. Since your marriage you've missed shifts and been in a number of accidents. Tuck in your shirt.

JOHN   (*overwrought*) I'm sorry sir. Mr. Castle, my marriage do not turn out the way I want. I'm afraid of my father-in-law.

KEITH   Afraid of that old man?

JOHN   Face to face, I meet him anytime but I'm afraid he waylay me sometime at night. He has a gun.

KEITH   Donald, d'you have any weapons in your possesion? Any guns?

DONALD   I've no gun sir, none at all.

KEITH   Heed me; if there are any further incidents between you men, I'll fire you both.

IRIS   One word from John about Donald's thefts here and he might be alive today.

KEITH   *(as himself)* But Castle had been told about the thefts.

                 EVELYN *enters as the aggrieved wife.*

EVELYN   Mr. Castle, I have gotten this letter in the mail and I think you should know of it.

KEITH   *(as CASTLE)* Young lady, you've been the cause of a lot of problems around here.

EVELYN   *(aggrieved)* "Dear Evelyn I am just writing you this note so as you can get wise to your so called husband. He certainly uses you as a sucker, there isn't a night but he has some woman standing behind him. All he took you for was so he could always have bond money but one of these days he will leave you flat, he is such a miserable dirty foreigner. I sure feel sorry for you." *(handing* KEITH/CASTLE *the letter)*

KEITH   You wrote this letter yourself.

EVELYN   I beg your pardon, I did not.

KEITH   There have been other 'anonymous' letters received here and this handwriting seems familiar. You've been warned before not to come around bothering the drivers. You've got quite a saucy reputation. Get off the property! You're nothing but trouble.

EVELYN	You want trouble? My father has been stealing from the Company for years and your boss knows it.
KEITH	I don't believe you.
EVELYN	Come down to the house some night Mr. Castle and you'll learn a few things.
KEITH	I would not be so foolish! (*ceases to be* CASTLE) Castle didn't believe her.
IRIS	She wasn't exactly a reliable source of information. Besides, what was he going to do -- repeat the allegation to his boss?
KEITH	Especially if his boss was riding Donald's golden trolley.
IRIS	John Dick was a threat to anybody who was on the take.

> *Change focus to* JOHN, EVELYN *and* ALEXANDRA. JOHN *is in his HSR uniform checking his leather satchel.*

JOHN	Thirty dollars is gone from my bond money.
EVELYN	Maybe you spent it?
JOHN	No. You got to lend me money, please.
ALEXANDRA	Spent it on those foreign women he meets on his streetcar.
JOHN	I will lose my job.
ALEXANDRA	Your bond money is your problem, Mr. Dick. You've touched me up for enough money already.
JOHN	(*to* EVELYN) Why you do this to me? You know I love you.

EVELYN	John, this is a big mistake. Just go away. Forget about me. Go back to your Annie.
JOHN	No! You swore before the mighty God to be my wife. If you don't be, then you must come to Court, all of you. (*exiting*)
ALEXANDRA	Yet another millstone, you've placed on our necks.

Change focus to IRIS *and* KEITH.

IRIS	Alexandra wanted John...gone.
KEITH	You're saying this murder was a family affair?
IRIS	Yes. You remember Anna Wolski?
KEITH	The widow lady, the one John dumped when he met Evelyn.
IRIS	She told me that the night before the murder, John came to see her;

Change focus to IRIS *as* ANNA *with* JOHN.

IRIS	(*as* ANNA) I had hopes, John, that one day you would marry me and be a father to my two girls.

JOHN *does not respond.*

IRIS	John, why you are crying?
JOHN	I am cry for myself, I am so worried for my life, that I might never see my family again. My own mother tell me not to go back to Hamilton because she feels that something bad will happen to me. If something does happen to me, go after Mr. and Mrs. MacLean and my wife. Anna, I believe in prayer and the Mighty God and he might somehow get me clear of this bunch, but if something happens to me, go after this bunch.

IRIS	Why do you not forget her, John?
JOHN	I love her, Anna.
IRIS	John, she is no good for you. She runs with other men. I see her myself with this guy Bohozuk in his Buick.
JOHN	Tomorrow I am go to meet her at Windsor Coffee Shop. She better start living with me or I get my revenge.
IRIS	(*as* ANNA) Vengeance is mine saith the Lord.
JOHN	Yes but I am his good right arm.

Change focus to KEITH *and* IRIS.

IRIS	(*as herself*) Whoever committed it, it's very possible Alexandra planned or encouraged the murder to protect her income and keep her daughter. It could have been the perfect crime if they'd have been more thorough in getting rid of the evidence.

Change focus to ALEXANDRA
being questioned.

WOOD	How did you heat your house?
ALEXANDRA	With a furnace, a coal furnace.
WOOD	Did you have to shovel it in or was it a stoker?
ALEXANDRA	Shovel it in.
WOOD	Who was looking after the ashes?
ALEXANDRA	Evelyn was. She attended the furnace.
WOOD	Did you observe her doing anything with ashes the week after the murder?

ALEXANDRA	Well, on Wednesday I was down in the basement washing and she started taking some ashes out to the alley. We normally had a lad come in to do that work, so I queried her but she ignored me.
WOOD	What quantity did she take out?
ALEXANDRA	Well, we had a rocker for the ashes, that was about two thirds full. She made two trips.
WOOD	What did she do then?
ALEXANDRA	She carried the ashes out and started spreading them by the garage doors and in the alleyway.
KEITH	She was always having her ashes hauled.

> *Change focus to* PRESTON *testifying.*

PRESTON	(*examing vial*) An analysis of ashes retrieved from the garage area at 32 Carrick reveals several small charred portions of bone matter and fragments of human teeth.

> EVELYN *sketches as* KEITH *peers over her shoulder.*

KEITH	(*grimacing*) While Preston was testifying, she was sketching teeth.
IRIS	Alexandra incriminates Evelyn but denies knowledge of the crematorium in her basement? Robinette wasn't letting her off so easily.
KEITH	What a cool customer -- Mr. J.J. Robinette, K.C.

> *Change focus to* IRIS / ROBINETTE *cross-examining* ALEXANDRA.

IRIS	(*as* Robinette) Mrs. McLean, you had a joint bank account with your husband?

ALEXANDRA	Yes, but the Street Railway have seized it.
IRIS	As the proceeds of your husband's thefts?
ALEXANDRA	So I understand.
IRIS	Has your own account been frozen.
ALEXANDRA	No.
IRIS	And it contains -- how much?
ALEXANDRA	(*quietly*) Some ten thousand dollars I believe.
IRIS	Ten thousand dollars! (*to* KEITH) Five years of Donald's salary! (*to* ALEX.) You own two houses, 214 Rosslyn and 32 Carrick?
ALEXANDRA	Carrick house is Evelyn's.
IRIS	Mrs. MacLean, you yourself were arrested in relation to these charges against your daughter, weren't you?
ALEXANDRA	Yes.
IRIS	You were kept in custody, where.
ALEXANDRA	The Barton Street jail.
IRIS	Not a very pleasant place. For how long?
ALEXANDRA	Thirteen days.
IRIS	Charged with what offence?
ALEXANDRA	Murder.
IRIS	Speak up, please, the jury can't hear you.
ALEXANDRA	Murder.

IRIS	But you were subsequently released?
ALEXANDRA	Yes.
IRIS	The charges were dropped?
ALEXANDRA	Yes.
IRIS	Were you in the witness room this morning?
ALEXANDRA	Yes.
IRIS	And then you were taken somewhere.
ALEXANDRA	I was taken into the Crown Attorney's office.
IRIS	How long were you in that office?
ALEXANDRA	Fifteen or twenty minutes.
IRIS	Was any inducement offered to you there?
ALEXANDRA	Oh, no.
IRIS	Any promises?
ALEXANDRA	Any promises?
IRIS	Mrs. MacLean! Did you make a bargain with anybody before you came in the box to give evidence today?
ALEXANDRA	No, no.
IRIS	(*as* ROBINETTE, *addressing the jury*) There is a woman on the hot seat. A woman with something to lose. How much does she know that she isn't telling? Who is she protecting? Herself? No one else can connect Evelyn to the ashes but her. That is your only source for the story of the ashes. The only source for the comments the accused is purported to have made about John being finished. A woman who was

IRIS

(*continued*) herself accused of this murder and had the charges dropped. A normal mother would go to any lengths to protect her daughter, but she seems more interested in keeping her own skirts clean.

> EVELYN *glares at her lawyer, twisting her mouth petulantly.* IRIS *ceases to be* ROBINETTE. WOOD *heaves a sigh.*

KEITH

Evelyn wasn't bothered that her mother testified against her; she was ticked off at Robinette for attacking Alexandra.

> ALEXANDRA *walks past* EVELYN *and their eyes meet.*

IRIS

There was a strange bond between them.

EVELYN

You look very nice mother, and you didn't break down.

ALEXANDRA

Who does your hair, dear?

EVELYN

One of the other girls is a hairdresser. (*brightening*) She's French. From Quebec.

ALEXANDRA

(*with distaste*) I've been trying to send you a new dress but the Governor of the Jail won't allow it. (*to* IRIS) She cares about her appearance, not like some.

IRIS

Imagine the house on Carrick Avenue that week after the murder;

KEITH

They couldn't have known how hard it was to burn a body. That's why they finally dumped the torso.

IRIS

Alexandra had to know what was going on, it was a charnel house; A dismembered body lying in the garage; the coal furnace blazing away, day and night burning the sawed-off limbs and

IRIS	(*continued*) severed head; the intolerable heat, the plumes of thick, black smoke oozing out the chimney; the smell of burning human flesh hanging like a pall upon the quiet middle-class street.
KEITH	You've been reading my stuff, haven't you? (*making another pass which* IRIS *is not so quick to parry*)
IRIS	In life as in literature, you need to learn subtlety.
KEITH	I thought maybe you'd want to concede defeat.
IRIS	Why ever would I?
KEITH	(*producing file*) Frank Boehler. The surprise eyewitness.
	Change focus *to* WOOD *and* PRESTON.
PRESTON	When the jury hears Boehler's story sir, they'll put her head back in the noose. I'd bet a week's pay.
WOOD	Do you play the ponies, Clarence?
PRESTON	Only if it's a sure thing, sir.
KEITH	He was a farmhand worked out on the Glanford Line on the day of the murder. (*reading file as* BOEHLER *on the stand*) I was scraping the sh— my boots off, when I heard two loud shots from a heavy calibre rifle or revolver. I served in the Army so I'm experienced with the sound of firearms. I picked up the milkers and headed for the barn when I hear a third shot. About half an hour later, I see this big man about 28 or 30 years old walking up past the drive shed. I asked him what he wanted. He said he got his car mired in a bog hole, in the mud down the road. So I hitched up the team, grabbed a rope and followed

KEITH	(*continued*) him down there. It was a big black car. There was a woman with dark hair behind the wheel. I seen a handbag and a package of cigarettes on her lap. There was a handle of a .32 calibre revolver was sticking out of the handbag. I told her to put the car in neutral and I (*hard 'g'*) gee'd the horses and pulled them out. As I went back to reclaim the rope, I seen part of a man's leg on the back seat, (*demonstrating*) the part below the knee, the calf and the foot. There was a black Oxford shoe on it and a black sock. The man was getting behind the wheel and as the woman slid over and I seen she threw a motorman's cap into the back. The big man said he had no money but he offered me a cigarette. I said, 'No thanks, I got cigarettes of my own.' (*pause*) Yes sir. Right there sir. The woman in the black dress -- Mrs. Evelyn Dick.
	EVELYN *glares at* KEITH *mouthing 'liar'.* WOOD *looksembarrassed.*
PRESTON	(*beaming,aside*) We've got 'er now, Inspector.
IRIS	(*as* ROBINETTE) Just a minute, Mr. Boehler. Very damning evidence, Mr. Boehler. When did you first tell this story to anyone?
KEITH	I don't know the date, sir.
IRIS	Who did you tell?
KEITH	Sergeant Preston, sir.
IRIS	When? A month ago perhaps?
KEITH	Two months ago.
IRIS	When you worked at the farm, did you take any newspaper?
KEITH	Yes.

IRIS	*The Hamilton Spectator,* in fact.
KEITH	Yes.
IRIS	And you can read?
KEITH	Yes.
IRIS	That trial was in October 1946. You did read about the first trial?
KEITH	Yes.
IRIS	Read about it quite carefully?
KEITH	I wouldn't say that, no. I read parts of it.
IRIS	Did you ever see a picture of Evelyn Dick?
KEITH	Yes sir.
IRIS	Of course you've seen pictures of Mrs. Dick. There have been lots of them around?
KEITH	Yes.
IRIS	Did you ever see pictures of Bill Bohozuk?
KEITH	Yes sir.
IRIS	And I suppose the man who was there, was Bill Bohozuk?
KEITH	Yes sir.
IRIS	You did not give any evidence at the first trial?
KEITH	No.
IRIS	You claim to have seen what you did, yet at no time did you breathe a word of this fantastic story to anyone for ten months?
KEITH	No, sir.

IRIS	And the first person you told this story to was Sergeant Preston?
KEITH	Well I told some fellow at a garage and it got back to Inspector Wood. He found me.
IRIS	You were in the army, Mr. Boehler?
KEITH	Yes sir, I am a veteran.
IRIS	How long did you serve?
KEITH	Five months and 28 days.
IRIS	How much of that time were you absent without leave?
KEITH	Gimme a minute..
IRIS	More than half that time, am I right?
	KEITH/BOEHLER *evades answering, ashamed.*
IRIS	When you were discharged from the Army, what was the reason?
KEITH	Medical.
IRIS	Clarify that, Mr. Boehler.
KEITH	Nervous.
IRIS	Nervous. There was a story in the newspaper that, as a result of your knowledge of this case, you were stabbed by a Chinaman?
KEITH	Yes, sir, they were after me.
IRIS	Any truth to that?
KEITH	Yes, he was either a Chinaman or a Jap.

IRIS	Where did this happen?
KEITH	In Hamilton, on Walnut Street.
IRIS	Where were you stabbed?
KEITH	I was not stabbed, sir.
IRIS	Did you not tell the police you were stabbed?
KEITH	I said I was attacked.
IRIS	How were you attacked?
KEITH	Well this fellow came toward me on the street and he asked me for a match. As I went to give him a light, he brought up his right hand (*demonstrating*) like this.
IRIS	What with, a gun?
KEITH	No a knife.
IRIS	You were stabbed then, were you?
KEITH	No, I was not stabbed.
IRIS	That is a very dramatic episode.(*rolling her eyes*) How did you ward that Chinaman off?
KEITH	I saw the knife and I knocked his hand aside like that (*demonstrating*) and the knife went through my leather windbreaker, through my sweater and my shirt.
IRIS	Did the police lay any charges?
KEITH	Not that I know of, sir.
IRIS	They didn't even bother to investigate, did they? (*as* KEITH/BOEHLER *squirms*) That is all, thank you. Gentlemen of the jury, I wouldn't convict a dog on this man's evidence.

WOOD	Clarence, I think your pony just pulled up lame.
	IRIS, *as* ROBINETTE, *passes* WOOD.
IRIS	(*smiling*) Hello, Charlie.
WOOD	J.J.
	KEITH *and* IRIS *cease being* BOEHLER *and* ROBINETTE. KEITH *puts down Boehler file.*
KEITH	(*feebly*) If even half of what he said was true..
IRIS	He'd still be a liar.
	Change focus *to* WOOD *and* PRESTON, *silently waiting. The sound of a door opening and many feet on a wooden floor.*
IRIS	"As the jury filed back, Evelyn, for the first time lost her composure, shaking with fright as she cast a strange, prolonged look at the men."
	EVELYN, *clutching her Bible, works the audience like the jury , as* KEITH *and* IRIS *read from their notes.*
KEITH	"The Whispering Gallery said 'They'll hang her'".
IRIS	(*from notes*) "It was one year to the day, to the hour of John Dick's murder as Evelyn faced the jury."
KEITH	(*from TRUE CRIME*) "In the press box, we watched the final drama unfold. We were minutes from deadlines and had wires open to city desks. The nation awaited, eagerly, fearfully."
IRIS	The clerk questions the foreman of the jury. The short sober-faced little man stood up and said;

KEITH   (*as* FOREMAN) "Not guilty of murder".

IRIS   (*handing her file to* KEITH) Touché.

                 Change focus to EVELYN *in*
                 PRESTON's *custody, raising her hands*
                 in triumph, smiling with joy and relief.

                 Change focus to WOOD *accepting*
                 the news stoically.

WOOD   Well, that's that. The jury has spoken.

                 Change focus to EVELYN *having a*
                 moment with the reporters.

EVELYN   I'll never be happier than today.

                 JOHN *watches* EVELYN *with mixed*
                 emotions and exits.

KEITH   I talked to Harold Foster, he's the cabbie who
                 drove her back and forth from Jail to Court. (*as*
                 FOSTER) After the verdict, she stood up there
                 and waved and smiled to us. I was glad to see her
                 get off. I don't believe for a moment she did it.

EVELYN   (*posing*) Make this a good one boys.

KEITH   (*as* FOSTER) Did you see her hands? Just like
                 doll hands. I don't believe she had any part in
                 cutting up a body. She promised me an
                 autographed picture.

IRIS   (*from notes*) A toothless crone advanced past me,
                 muttering and clutching a bag of rotten fruit to
                 throw. Others pitched frozen mud. A young man
                 threw her a bouquet of red roses...

                 KEITH *puts roses at* EVELYN's *feet*
                 but PRESTON *restrains her from*
                 picking them up.

KEITH	(*as himself*)...but she could not pick them up. She was still a prisoner charged with murder.
	KEITH *gives* IRIS *the roses.*
WOOD	Evelyn Dick you are hereby charged under Section 259 of the Criminal Code that sometime in the two years following September 5, 1944, you did murder your infant son, Peter David White MacLean.
IRIS	When did they find...
KEITH	The third time they searched 32 Carrick.
	Change focus *to* PRESTON *searching and* ALEXANDRA *watching him.*
PRESTON	Mrs. MacLean, there are some suitcases and a cabin trunk in the attic. Have you the keys?
ALEXANDRA	(*co-operatively*) No, Sergeant, I have none. Evelyn has them at the Jail, in her key case.
	PRESTON *exits and* DONALD *arrives, flushed and out of breath.*
ALEXANDRA	I see you're the worse for drink.
DONALD	(*panicky*) Hae they cops been here snoopin' about?
ALEXANDRA	Yes. They just left.
DONALD	Ha' they been upstairs t'the attic?
ALEXANDRA	Yes. They asked for the key of the suitcases.
DONALD	D'they open them?
ALEXANDRA	No.

A pause as they look at each other with complicity.

DONALD   Gie us a hammer an' a chisel, willye?

> **Change focus** *to* WOOD *and* PRESTON.

PRESTON   When I returned to 32 Carrick, I found that in my absence, the cabin trunk had been broken into and was now empty.

WOOD   (*displeased*) We'll never know what was in that trunk.

PRESTON   Three of the suitcases had nothing in them. The fourth was quite heavy, forty to fifty pounds.

> **Change focus** *to* PRESTON *and* ALEXANDRA *with suitcase on kitchen table.*

PRESTON   Whose suitcase is this?

ALEXANDRA   Evelyn's.

PRESTON   What is in it?

ALEXANDRA   Schoolbooks and Evelyn's things.

PRESTON   When did you last see it open?

ALEXANDRA   A few months ago.

PRESTON   It's locked. Do you have a key?

ALEXANDRA   No, I do not.

PRESTON   Are you sure?

ALEXANDRA   Yes.

PRESTON   Have you any tools about?

ALEXANDRA   Yes. (*indicating*)

>PRESTON *takes the hammer and screwdriver and 'jimmies' the lock. He opens the case, winces at the smell, and closes it quickly.* ALEXANDRA *reacts with horror.*

>**Change focus** *to to* KEITH *and* IRIS.

KEITH   Evelyn found herself pregnant three times. Heather in 1942, a stillborn baby in '43 and Peter David White born September 5th, 1944.

PRESTON   (*reading evidence from notebook*) As soon as I opened the lid, I noticed a very strange odour. There was a burlap bag overtop of a cardboard box which was placed in a wicker meat hamper. I lifted off the bag and opened the cardboard box and I saw a block of cement with fabric and a khaki skirt sticking through it. (*holding up the Red Cross skirt*) The waistband of the skirt protruded from the cement. It was a Red Cross uniform skirt. There was a tag on it which read 'Firth Brother's Quality Tailors, E. MacLean'.

KEITH   She had a custom-made uniform but she never belonged to the Red Cross.

IRIS   The story of her life; she never belonged.

PRESTON   (*testifying*) I used a chisel and a hammer and proceeded to chop away the cement. As I did I discovered a little leatherette shopping bag. It was zippered shut. I opened the zipper. There I discovered the decomposed body of an infant. It was still clothed but the fabric was rotted. In the remains of the diaper we found a small piece of surgical gauze like the dressing used on a newly circumsized male infant.

WOOD	That child must have died within a day of leaving the hospital.

KEITH *and* IRIS *peer in the suitcase.*

PRESTON	The body was in a state of mummification which means the tissues were drying up, so brittle they came apart on handling. A loop of hemp twine was tied about the throat. The circumference of the loop was about five inches. The circumference of the neck of a normal newborn is seven to nine inches.
IRIS	I cannot see a mother killing a child this way.
KEITH	Don't be sentimental. What was she gonna do? Put it out on an ice flow in the Bay?
PRESTON	In the suitcase there is a compartment under the lid, a fabric pocket if you will. In it I found the photograph of a baby. The photograph of an infant.
IRIS	(*studying* EVELYN) Why would she take a photograph of a baby she didn't intend to keep?]

Change focus to WOOD, PRESTON *and* EVELYN.

WOOD	Tell me, does Bohozuk have anything to do with this baby?
EVELYN	My lawyer said not to talk so don't tell him I said anything. In September of 1944, the fifth I think, I gave birth to a baby boy at the Mountain Hospital. It was the spit of Bohozuk. It had dark hair and weighed nine pounds, two ounces. The day I left hospital, I met Bill at The Royal Connaught Hotel. When I got into his two-tone Buick he said, "Give him to me. I'll get rid of the little bastard" and he strangled it right there by knotting a blanket around its neck. He put it in a zipper bag and took it away with him.

EVELYN   (*continued*) Later he brought it back to me in a
                box, a cardboard box. He said for me to keep it
                till they started the rowing again. He would take
                it out in the Bay then, and, you know, get rid of
                it.

WOOD   How did your skirt come to be stuck in the
                cement?

EVELYN   The box was leaking when I got it back from
                Bohozuk and I used the skirt to stop the cement
                from running all over everything.

WOOD   You mean the cement was wet?

EVELYN   Yes and I didn't want it to get all over the
                suitcase.

WOOD   Did you put the cement in?

EVELYN   No, sir, I had no cement in my home.

WOOD   Where did you live before you went to the
                hospital?

EVELYN   On Rosslyn Street. My father said I couldn't
                bring the baby back there. He wanted no more
                children in the house.

IRIS   (*pointing to* DONALD) There's a man with a
                motive to kill the baby.

PRESTON   (*holding solid bag of cement and trowel, aside to*
                WOOD) This bag of cement and the trowel, I
                found in the basement of Donald MacLean's
                home.

WOOD   (*examining suitcase*) No man who works with
                his hands would mix cement like that. That's a
                woman's work.

                Change focus *to* KEITH *and* IRIS.

KEITH	Bohozuk wasn't the father. Evelyn said, herself, that the night they went to The Tivoli was the first time she had sex relations with Bill.
IRIS	A year after Peter was born.
KEITH	Right.
IRIS	I believe Evelyn lied about Bill being the father but I can't imagine her killing the child.
KEITH	Why not?
IRIS	Perhaps it's that baby picture.
KEITH	Listen; Samuel Henson owns Henson Park Manor. When Evelyn as 'Mrs. Norman White' came to him in search of an apartment, she said she was pregnant but the baby -- I think she said that she was under medical examination and the baby was dead. She was going into the hospital to have it removed. Surely that indicates her intent.
IRIS	Evelyn would say anything to get that apartment. Any landlord knowing she was to have two children might refuse to rent to her. I'd lie in that situation. But why not get rid of the suitcase?
KEITH	Was she blackmailing someone? Maybe the real father of baby Peter? There's something in one of Alexandra's statements. (*rifling through papers*)

Change focus to ALEXANDRA
being questioned.

WOOD	Was Norman White a real or fictitious person?
ALEXANDRA	I believe he was a real person.
WOOD	Did you think Evelyn was married to him?
ALEXANDRA	Yes.

WOOD	Did she tell you that?
ALEXANDRA	Yes.
WOOD	Was that true?
ALEXANDRA	No.
WOOD	But she went under the name of Mrs. Norman White?
ALEXANDRA	Yes.
WOOD	Whom did Evelyn say was the father of Heather?
ALEXANDRA	Norman White.
WOOD	Did she ever mention one Angus McIntosh?
ALEXANDRA	No.
WOOD	A gentleman, now deceased who lived in the city?
ALEXANDRA	No.
KEITH	Angus McIntosh was an old man who made a fortune during the war with the production of armoured plate. He died during the trial, supposedly of 'natural causes'. (*miming shooting himself*)
WOOD	Do you have a bank account?
ALEXANDRA	Yes.
WOOD	How much is in it?
ALEXANDRA	Around ten thousand dollars.
WOOD	How much of that came from Evelyn?
ALEXANDRA	Around six thousand dollars.

WOOD	In what size sums did she give you money?
ALEXANDRA	Fifty or one hundred dollars at a time.
WOOD	Did your daughter work?
ALEXANDRA	No.
WOOD	When did this money begin to come from her?
ALEXANDRA	A few years ago.
WOOD	Did it come more rapidly after the birth of Heather?
ALEXANDRA	Yes.
KEITH	Aha!
WOOD	Who did the money come from?
ALEXANDRA	I don't know.
IRIS	Angus McIntosh?
KEITH	Bingo!

> WOOD *puts the suitcase in front of* ALEXANDRA.

WOOD	You're familiar with this suitcase?
ALEXANDRA	Yes.
WOOD	When your daughter went to the Mountain Hospital last year, did she take it with her?
ALEXANDRA	She did.
WOOD	Did she return with it?
ALEXANDRA	Aye.

WOOD	And it was during this confinement when Baby Peter White was born?
ALEXANDRA	I knew it was a boy. I never knew its name.
WOOD	When Evelyn returned from the Mountain Hospital, after the birth of that baby, was she alone?
ALEXANDRA	Yes, she told me that she had put the little boy up for adoption through the Children's Aid. I took her at her word.
WOOD	Did you see this suitcase in the Henson Park apartment?
ALEXANDRA	Yes.
WOOD	And later, in the attic on Carrick Street where Sgt. Preston seized it?
ALEXANDRA	Yes.
WOOD	What did you think was in that suitcase?
ALEXANDRA	Evelyn told me it was just her school things.

Change focus to IRIS *and* KEITH.

KEITH	Evelyn moves a dead baby from one house to another and keeps a picture of it. (*shuddering*) - why? - for blackmail?
IRIS	No. Evelyn could have had an emotional need to keep that baby, especially if she didn't kill it.
KEITH	She killed it because one more kid would cramp her style.
IRIS	(*snapping*) You think having a baby is like going in for an oil change. Listen. (*reading from a file*) This nurse was in charge of the maternity ward. "Mrs. White had a private room with a

IRIS	(*continued*) phone and a goodly supply of funds." Can you smell the jealousy? (*reading*) "I cannot recall seeing any male visitors which was a matter of some discussion." I'll just bet it was! They knew, the whole ward. All her money couldn't hide the truth - the baby was illegitimate! She sent herself flowers. Listen, "Mrs. White spoke often of her mother who was unable to visit her." Not one visitor did she have -- not even her mother. "However she appeared very fond of the baby boy, undertaking all of his regular feedings." For ten days, all Evelyn has in the world is this baby boy. How could she strangle it after that? Any woman forced to give up a baby because it was...a bastard, might keep a picture of her child, long after.

> KEITH *intuits her meaning and hands her* CELESTE's *picture.*

KEITH	And she might even call her, 'her niece'?
IRIS	My daughter. Celeste.

> KEITH *is abashed and moved.*

KEITH	You sent yourself flowers? (*pause*) Miss Muirson, I'm sorry.

> *After a moment,* IRIS *acknowledges his apology. A thought suddenly occurs to* KEITH.

KEITH	Alexandra knew what was in the suitcase.
IRIS	When did she say that?
KEITH	(*looking for the file*) At the preliminary hearing on the charge of murdering the baby, laid against Bohozuk.
IRIS	But that was a closed hearing. No reporters allowed.

KEITH	(*holding up his prize file*) Eat your heart out, Dave Woodruff.
IRIS	He hasn't got one. How'd you get that?
KEITH	I took somebody to Eva's for the special.
IRIS	Eva's?
KEITH	By The Steel Company Gates.
IRIS	What's the special?
KEITH	Two beers and a (*clucking*) for a buck.
IRIS	The things you can do for a dollar in Hamilton.
KEITH	So Bohozuk's lawyer, was a feisty bugger by the name of Schreiber. He had a limp. Now the only evidence linking Bohozuk to the baby was Evelyn's testimony. Shreiber went for the throat.

> *Change focus to* EVELYN's *cross examination.* KEITH *plays* SCHREIBER. EVELYN *pushes the Bible away, refusing to testify.*

KEITH	She refused to testify but when the Judge threatened her with contempt she relented. (*as* SCHREIBER *to* EVELYN *who picks up Bible*) Is there a Norman White?
EVELYN	Yes.
KEITH	Was he your husband?
EVELYN	No.
KEITH	On the birth certificate, did you give his name as the father of this child, Peter David White?
EVELYN	Yes.

KEITH	Why then do you state that Bill Bohozuk was the father?
EVELYN	Because he was responsible for getting me pregnant.
KEITH	How do you know?
EVELYN	Because he was the only one.
KEITH	Careful. Were you having sex relations with Norman White?
EVELYN	No.
KEITH	Well why give White's name?
EVELYN	Because Bill did not want to be involved.
KEITH	You have had three illegitimate children, correct?
EVELYN	Yes.
KEITH	The little girl Heather, a stillborn baby and this infant that you say Bohozuk took away and returned to you, dead, in a cardboard box which you put in a suitcase.
EVELYN	Yes.
KEITH	Did your mother know what was in the box?
EVELYN	Yes, I told her.
KEITH	Whose idea was it to get rid of this child?
EVELYN	Bohozuk's.
KEITH	On September 5th, 1944 when this baby was born, Bill Bohozuk hadn't even met you.

EVELYN   Bill is the one who got me pregnant. I went into
              a store to do some shopping and had been
              drinking and he took advantage of me.

KEITH   How many times have you been taken advantage
              of in your life?

EVELYN   Three times.

KEITH   Are you serious? Haven't there been many men?

EVELYN   A few.

KEITH   Quite a few. How many?

EVELYN   I don't know.

KEITH   Who were you keeping steady company with at
              the time this baby was conceived?

EVELYN   No one, sir.

KEITH   You did not keep company with a man in the
              city for two years, 1943 and 1944?

EVELYN   No. I'm positive.

KEITH   Around the time this child was conceived?

EVELYN   No sir!

KEITH   He's a married man. I must mention his name.
              David Holmes-Webster.

IRIS   David!

EVELYN   Yes.

KEITH   Is it not a fact that the father of that child could
              have been any one of a hundred men in this city?

EVELYN   I beg your pardon, not that many.

KEITH	How many then?
EVELYN	I can't remember.

> EVELYN *'clams up'*. KEITH *turns to* IRIS *and hands her the file.*

KEITH	*(as himself)* Again the Judge threatened Evelyn with contempt if she didn't answer — so she did.
IRIS	*(reading)* A Doctor...
EVELYN	Yes.
IRIS	...the merchant banker...
EVELYN	Yes.
IRIS	...partner in the firm of...
EVELYN	Yes.
IRIS	...Robinson's Department Store?
EVELYN	Yes.
IRIS	A gentleman? Wing Commander? King's Councillor? Canada Life Assurance? A jockey? A fireman?
EVELYN	Yes.
KEITH	*(as SCHREIBER)* Any other names come to mind?
EVELYN	The Judge's son for one.
KEITH	*(as himself)* The old bugger only dropped his pencil! Then he immediately slapped a gag order on the jury. They sure as hell didn't want those names bandied about but they were all over town in a week. Once she got started they couldn't shut her up. There were suicides in the Southwest.

KEITH	(*as* SHREIBER) Did you buy silver engraved cigarette cases at Birks and give them to all of your male friends?
EVELYN	Just two.
KEITH	You have been running around with various men since you were 15 years old?
EVELYN	I beg your pardon, I have not.
KEITH	You really mean that seriously?
EVELYN	Yes, sir.
KEITH	When the police spoke to you on the first occasion after the discovery of the child I understand you never mentioned Bohozuk at all.
EVELYN	Yes, sir, I did.
KEITH	Did you not mention the name of another person responsible for the birth of Baby Peter?
EVELYN	No, sir.
KEITH	Didn't you state that your father was the father of this baby?
EVELYN	No, sir, I did not.
KEITH	You would of course lie now, to protect your father.
EVELYN	No, sir.
	KEITH *ceases to be* SHREIBER. ***Change focus*** *to* KEITH *and* IRIS.
IRIS	Incest. Of course.
KEITH	She wouldn't sleep with that. (*pointing to* DONALD)

IRIS	Why do you presume she had a choice? If Donald was the father of baby Peter, that's why he lived in the cellar and Evelyn slept in her mother's bed. For protection. That sex relationship could have been going on for a long time. There's a young woman I've met socially. No names. She and Evelyn were friends in Grade School. She told me when she was eleven or twelve, she was invited to spend a weekend at the MacLean house. At night, in bed, Evelyn made sexual advances to her. The girl refused but Evelyn was very insistent. Scared the poor kid out of her wits.
KEITH	Lots of kids fool around at that age.
IRIS	This was different. She said it was only after she was married that she understood what Evelyn was doing that night.
KEITH	She grew up fast.
IRIS	Yes, because Evelyn had already been introduced to sex by her father.
KEITH	Whew.
IRIS	It explains her lies and fantasies, her use of sex to show affection. Now, who would have the greater motive to get rid of the baby -- her or her parents?
KEITH	Whoa! Iris, leave the speculation to *True Crime*.
IRIS	Remember what the shrink said? "When we talked about the woman's early life, especially her life with her parents, it distressed her deeply. She cried like a baby. This was the only time I saw it happen."

KEITH	Evelyn denied that Donald was the father of the baby. And even if she said he was, why believe her? Donald could have slept in the basement because he was a drunk or because he liked his dog better than his wife. (*pause*) I can feature that. But even if he did father the baby, Evelyn could have protected it or given it up for adoption.
IRIS	Yes. Who am I kidding? She might have done it. Infanticide does occur -- too often with illegitimate children.
KEITH	(*as* JUDGE) Stand up Evelyn Dick.
	Change focus *to* EVELYN *rising to face the* JUDGE.
KEITH	(*as* JUDGE) You have been convicted of a horrible crime. I see nothing whatsoever that justifies me in extending mercy to you. You must be sentenced to the maximum term that I am allowed to impose. The sentence of this Court, is that you shall spend the rest of your natural life in penitentiary.
IRIS	Life imprisonment. This punishment is for being acquitted of John Dick's murder.
KEITH	(*as himself*) Nothing happens in a vacuum. The Judge thought she'd gotten away with one murder already.
	JOHN *reappears to watch* EVELYN.
KEITH	Bill Bohozuk is probably the happiest guy in town tonight.
IRIS	It's not every day you're acquitted of two murders.

KEITH	He'll probably take a couple of weeks off and go back to his old job in the plant. I'll bet he thinks twice about picking up strange skirt from now on.
	Change focus *to* WOOD *and* PRESTON.
WOOD	Well, Clarence, that's the end of that horse race.
PRESTON	Maybe the end of the court cases but here in Hamilton, they'll be talking about the Torso Murder for years.
WOOD	I'd rather they remember my wins than my shows. Pleasure working with you.
PRESTON	Where you off to next?
WOOD	A murder in St. Catharines. Another strange one, we've got no body but we got a killer. He'll swing. I am not losing two in a row. You?
PRESTON	I'm back to Morality, kickin' in porch doors of blind pigs and rounding up the gambling chinks.
WOOD	Stay away from the ponies, Clarence. (*stopping*) She certainly put us through our paces, didn't she?.
	WOOD *pauses to look at* EVELYN, *then exits.*
	Change focus *to* PRESTON *hanfcuffing* DONALD.
DONALD	Has she sent any word for me, ma wee pet?
	PRESTON *shakes his head.*
DONALD	I had nothing to do with Dick's murder. I only wanted to help her, Clarence, help ma own kith and kin. That's why I pleaded guilty.

PRESTON	(*bitterly*) You're an accessory, Donald, to a murder that, it seems, nobody committed.
	DONALD *cuffed to* PRESTON, *looks at* ALEXANDRA *and* EVELYN.
DONALD	I lost my daughter, the only thing I ever loved. (*to* ALEXANDRA) How did the two of us, make something as beautiful as her? (*exits*)
EVELYN	(*to* ALEXANDRA) He belongs in jail or in the bug house.
	Change focus *to* ALEXANDRA *rising to speak to* IRIS.
ALEXANDRA	I have something I want to put in the papers. People have the wrong impression that I testified against my daughter. I merely told the truth as I was sworn to do. Heather and I receive an awful lot of sympathetic mail and no matter how busy I am, I always take time to read the letters. However, on Friday I received 18 anonymous phone calls. No lady or person of refinement would place those. Some of them even questioned my fitness as a mother.
	ALEXANDRA *exits.*
	Change focus *to* IRIS *and* KEITH *alone.*
IRIS	Why would The Children's Aid allow her to raise Heather? That's a crime.
	KEITH *is ripping up his rough draft.*
IRIS	What are you doing?
KEITH	I thought I had this whole story in the bag but I'll have to start over. You win.

IRIS	It's too late to matter, anyway. Too bad she had the family she did — given a chance, who knows what she might`ve been?
KEITH	Oh, God, I'm bushed. How 'bout you?
IRIS	Yes. I was just thinking about David Holmes-Webster keeping Evelyn as a mistress. I thought I knew him.
KEITH	Who knows what evil lurks in the hearts of men? The Shadow knows...

> IRIS's *telephone rings and she answers.*

IRIS	Hello. Yes, this is Iris Muirson. What time is it? Four a.m. No, don't bother making the call operator, the deadline's passed. Thanks anyway. Oh yes, your theory...(*listening*) Oh! Thank you very much!

> IRIS *hangs up and* KEITH *watches eagerly.*

IRIS	She says Boehler did it with Bohozuk's gun in Romanelli's car. And her cousin used to live on Carrick Street so it must be true.
KEITH	My head hurts. Do you want to have breakfast? Claim your winnings?

> IRIS *crosses to the door, and puts on coat and hat.*

IRIS	Sure. Where shall we go?
KEITH	The Royal Connaught?
IRIS	Good.

> IRIS *turns at the door as* KEITH *packs up the box.*

IRIS   They have excellent room service.

                       IRIS *exits.* KEITH *stops, thinks, and*
                       his eyes brighten.

KEITH   Ah! Subtlety. (*running after her and exiting*)

                       Change focus *to* EVELYN *alone.*

EVELYN   What are they saying about me out there? Are
                       there any good mentions? All I ever wanted was
                       to make things happy and bright, to have some
                       good times...so...make this a good one boys.

                       EVELYN *strikes her last pose for the*
                       cameras.

                       Black.

                       The End.

HISTORICAL AND BIOGRAPHICAL NOTES

Physical descriptions of the characters are found in the front of the book and within the stage directions in the script. These notes are to provide some historical background and context to aid the performer in preparing a role.

Evelyn Grant MacLean was an only child, born in Grimsby, Ontario on October 4, 1920. The MacLeans were recent immigrants from Scotland. At the time, they were attempting to farm but, within a year of their daughter's birth, they gave it up and moved to Hamilton. Her father, Donald, soon went to work for the Hamilton Street Railway (H.S.R.) and remained with the company until his arrest on charges of stealing money from it, in 1946. In the early years, he was a uniformed driver and conductor. One might speculate upon the relationship of her father's occupation to Evelyn's later predilection for picking up HSR drivers. Long before she met John Dick, she was known to have, in the words of a gentlemanly old dispatcher, "a soft spot for the drivers". However, at some point in the early 1930's, Donald MacLean left the streetcars and took a janitorial position at the HSR car barns and offices, located near Wentworth and King Streets in Hamilton. This position paid less but certainly offered other lucrative possibilities as documented in the script: access to the company vault and the fareboxes. For years, he was a fixture in the beverage room of the Balmoral Tavern, next door to the HSR yard. Her mother, Alexandra, so far as we know, was never employed in Canada. Money was never a problem to the MacLeans again.

The MacLeans had a two-bedroom brick bungalow constructed at 214 Rosslyn Street around 1924. At some point, Donald moved from the bedroom to the basement of the house and remained in residence there until the day of his arrest. Alexandra moved into Evelyn's bedroom and for the remainder of their life together, wherever they dwelt, mother and daughter shared a bed.

Evelyn was educated at various schools, including Loretto Academy (although she was not a Catholic) and Westdale Collegiate, neither of which were in her neighbourhood. As as a young girl, she was lonely, sexually precocious, polite, and so quiet she often went unnoticed.

The MacLeans had an unhappy and disputatious marriage by all accounts, separating seven times before June of 1945 when Alexandra moved with Evelyn and Heather to the apartment which Evelyn had kept at Henson Park Manor, 316 James Street South. Subsequently, the three moved to the house at 32 Carrick Street where John Dick lived with them for a brief time.

As a young girl, in order to win friends at school, Evelyn often bought treats and toys for those she liked, items paid for from a purse which was always full of change. This tactic did not succeed, apparently. At a time when the monied class was under the constraints of the depression, the wealth of the janitor's daughter often provoked resentment rather than acceptance.

As Evelyn grew older, she lavished silver cigarette cases and tailored suits on the men who caught her fancy. This met with somewhat greater success, at least in the short term. She began to develop her flamboyant streak, in dress and demeanour, blossoming into a beautiful young woman with expensive taste and a penchant for the fast life. As an example, Evelyn was a regular on the thoroughbred racing circuit. At a meet in Fort Erie she encountered Mr. and Mrs. Powers, a couple who were her neighbours on Rosslyn Street. When Mrs. Powers remarked that they would have to go back to Hamilton after the races because they were unable to get a hotel room, Evelyn gave them a key and said, "Here, take my room. I won't be needing it, I'm sleeping with a jockey."

Evelyn's profligate lifestyle was supported largely by her father's thefts although she apparently received money from certain men with whom she became sexually involved. One such man was a member of a prominent Canadian brewing family who trained with the R.C.A.F. at their base in Mount Hope, just outside Hamilton.

At one time she became engaged to the scion of a wealthy family, according to a magazine report, but the wedding never took place. To explain her daughter, Heather, born in 1941, Evelyn invented a husband she named Norman White, conveniently at sea with the Royal Canadian Navy, and until her marriage to John, she referred to herself as Mrs. Norman White.

Heather was often referred to as a mongoloid but she was neither a Down Syndrome child, nor retarded. However, Heather did have an Oriental cast to her facial features. The identity of her father is unknown but it seems that he did contribute financially to Heather's upbringing, whether voluntarily or by blackmail, it is impossible to say.

In considering the question of illegitimacy in the 1940's, one cannot underestimate the stigma attached to such a condition. In addition, the Children's Aid Society had sweeping and arbitrary powers to intervene in the lives of children born out of wedlock. Evelyn's masquerade was probably not uncommon among unmarried mothers.

John Dick was born in New Halbstadt, Ekaterinoslay, Russia, on May 25th 1906. Various groups of the Mennonite Bretheren had emigrated there from Germany in an attempt to escape religious persecution and to settle new agricultural communities. John's family was from Silesia, a province in the south-east corner of Prussia, part of the old German Empire.

He and his family emigrated to Canada in 1924. Members of the Mennonite sect to which he belonged were not the "Orthodox", if you will, but they would have spoken High German as their first language at home and at church. John left the fruit farm near Beamsville and worked as a driver for Fearman's Meat Packers before joining the HSR. He was keeping company with Anna Wolski when he met Evelyn. Within a month of that meeting, they had married. Only then did he begin to learn the truth about his bride.

Clarence Preston was of British origin as were so many of the police officers of his day. He was a cop from the old school and worked on the Morality Squad for a number of years before he was rotated onto Homicide. He finished his career with the Hamitlon Police Department in the Fifties without advancing beyond the rank of Sergeant.

Charles Wood was an excellent criminal investigator whose career spanned fifty years, from the rum-running Twenties till his retirement in the mid-Seventies. He handled a great number of difficult and high profile cases, including the investigation of Rocco Perri himself, in the 1920's. Certainly when he was assigned to the Dick case, he was at the height of his career.

Donald MacLean was sentenced to two concurrent five-year prison terms — one for theft and one for being an accessory after the fact. Upon his release he returned to Hamilton. Estranged from Alexandra, he eked out a living as a parking-lot attendant until his death in 1955. I was told by a journalist that he offered three thousand dollars in cash to Donald in exchange for the true story of what had happened to John Dick. Donald refused in spite of the fact that he was living in penury.

Alexandra MacLean remained in Hamilton and raised Heather. From what I have been able to ascertain, she never again saw Evelyn after her incarceration in the Kingston Penitentiary for Women. Alexandra MacLean died in 1959.

Evelyn Dick served twelve years for the murder of her son and was paroled in 1958. She turned down a lucrative offer for her life story from *Weekend Magazine*, remarried and as of this writing, lives somewhere in Ontario under an assumed name. In 1985, the federal cabinet granted her a rarely used, ancient form of pardon called a Royal Perogative of Mercy which freed the former Evelyn Dick from having to report to a Parole Officer and allowed her to collect a Canada Pension.

Heather Maria Moorehead, Evelyn's daughter, married, divorced and left Hamilton around 1970. Her whereabouts are unknown.

Bill Bohozuk was acquitted of the charges of murdering John Dick and the infant, Peter David White. He remained in Hamilton and resumed his old job at Dominion Foundries. His first wife, Helen returned to Canada to testify on his behalf but after Bill's acquittal she once again left him. He changed his name, presumably because of his notoriety, remarried in 1954 and presently lives in retirement on Hamilton Mountain.

Anna Wolski attended Evelyn's trials faithfully. She remarried a few years later and ironically was, herself, murdered by her husband in 1953.

John J. Robinette went on to become one of Canada's leading lawyers and a noted expert on constitutional law with the firm of McCarthy & McCarthy. He retired in 1990 at the age of 84.

—Douglas Rodger